ASTEROIDS IN MIDPOINTS, ASPECTS AND PLANETARY PICTURES

BOOKS BY EMMA BELLE DONATH:

Approximate Positions of Asteroids, 1900-1999
Approximate Positions of Asteroids, 1851-2050
Asteroids in the Birth Chart
Asteroids in the Birth Chart, revised
Asteroids in Midpoints, Aspects and Planetary Pictures
Asteroids in Synastry
Asteroids in the U.S.A.
Minor Aspects Between Natal Planets
Have We Met Before?
Relocation

ASTEROIDS IN MIDPOINTS

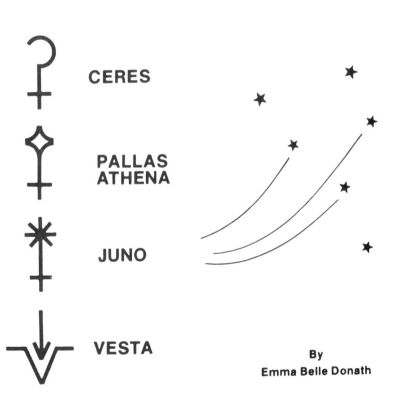

CERES

PALLAS
ATHENA

JUNO

VESTA

By
Emma Belle Donath

First Printing 1982
Second Printing 1988
ISBN Number: 0-86690-242-2
Library of Congress Number: 83-71149

Cover design: Anne Marie Bush

Published by:
American Federation of Astrologers, Inc.
P.O. Box 22040, 6535 South Rural Road
Tempe, Arizona 85282

Printed in the United States of America

"..............in the process of spiritual attainment, the feminine principle must first be lifted and restored from its fall..."

Corinne Heline
New Age Bible Interpretation,
New Testament, Vol. V, page 42
Published by New Age Press, Inc.
4636 Vineta Avenue
La Canada, CA 91011*

CONTENTS

PREFACE

This book completes a five-volume report on the astrological validity of asteroids Ceres, Pallas Athena, Juno and Vesta begun in the fall of 1974. These volumes present research material about the four major planetoids in progressively more complex terms. All of the information can be correlated by serious students or teachers; beginning astrologers may wish to use only the house and sign positions of *Asteroids in the Birth Chart, revised.* In addition there is traditional aspect material included in the first chapter of this book which may be of interest to beginning and intermediate astrologers.

Very little instruction is given herein concerning specific techniques of cosmobiology and the Uranian, or Hamburg School, of Astrology, because excellent texts are available detailing both procedures. References of these books are mentioned in the various chapters and appendices of this book. Thus, astrologers familiar with multiple methods of delineation need not read through pages of preliminary explanations in order to learn the testing procedures applied in the research reported here.

Over one-half of the delineations presented are from natal horoscopes. The other information contains data observed from combinations of progressions, directions and transits. In natal research no orb of over one and one-half degrees was allowed, even with the Sun or the Moon. Events found by transit or directions were calculated to seconds of accuracy. Only planetary relationships are listed or considered. No speculations were made about which set of rulerships applied in any case reported herein. Additional information may thus be determined by practicing astrologers knowing their particular clients.

Every midpoint combination listed in this book comes from events verified either by historical facts or by confirmation by the individual whose horoscope was being tested. Many of the delineations were repeated in dozens of charts. Some rare medical conditions, such as rupture of the colon, happened in multiple cases of the author's own clients during the years of research. During one particular year three cases of Baker's cyst were brought to my attention and all proved to have the same planetary picture with Ceres involvement. Numerous other such incidents happened to confirm delineations presented in this volume.

ix

Asteroid positions in the horoscopes were calculated from either *The Asteroid Ephemeris*, by Dobyns, Pottenger and Michelsen, or by Astro-Computing Services, San Diego, California. Visible planets and personal points were calculated from positions given in *The American Ephemeris*, by Michelsen, by Astro-Computing Services, or on the PET Commodore System with Matrix software. Transneptunian points or planets were computed from the positions in *Uranian Astrology Guide and Ephemeris*, by Sherman and Frank; or from the *Transneptunian Ephemeris*, by Michelsen.

Many other astrologers have assisted in this research. Some have shared charts and data while others have aided in laboriously compiling lists of midpoints, planetary pictures and exact aspects. Thanks to the following people for all measure of support in preparing this volume: Lois Daton, Liz Kelly, Barbara Vaughn, Franscoise Dworschak, and Susan Bricker of Dayton, Ohio; Myriam Ruthchild of Pomeroy, Ohio; Toni McDonald of Orlando, Florida; Wilayne Clawson of Romulus, Michigan; Darlene Enber and Reva Fitterman of Chicago, Illinois; my husband Robert Charles Donath and scores of others who helped in large and small ways.

My special gratitude goes to John Robert Hawkins of Dallas, Texas, who has graciously prepared a lengthy foreword for use in both this book and the revised edition of *Asteroids in the Birth Chart*. In discussing the printing the foreword, "Why Should the Asteroids Rule the Sign of Virgo?," in two of the five volumes we both felt that astrologers whose primary interest was in the field of either cosmobiology or Uranian Astrology might have the opportunity to read this material only through its inclusion in this particular volume of the series. John has done extensive research with the major asteroids with interesting results. Hopefully he will, in time, publish further material about these little planetoids. Meanwhile, John Hawkin's book, *Transpluto, or Should We Call Him Bacchus, the Ruler of Taurus?*, fills an important gap in information about an outer planet of our solar system.

The most important reason for publishing this, or any other volume containing basic research material, is to excite other astrologers to use the new concepts and ideas in their own counseling or research. It is only through sharing information that we begin to understand other facets of the heavens about us and eventually other parts of our own personalities. Just because a delineation is printed does not make it the gospel about a particular combination of planetary energies. Investigation of the asteroids is still in the toddler stage and needs thousands of hours of further consideration before any theories or findings will be accepted into the older body of astrological knowledge. But there must be a beginning, such as Eleanor Bach's publication of the *Ephemeris of the Asteroids Ceres, Pallas, Juno, Vesta, 1900-2000* in 1973; Esther V. Leinbach's comprehensive books, entitled *Planets and Asteroids* and *Transits*, published in 1974 and 1976; articles and a daily ephemeris written by Dr. Zipporah Dobyns; and this little series of my books.

Now Mark Pottenger has perfected a computer program for finding accurate asteroid placements over the centuries, Digicomp has incorporated the asteroid positions into their basic computers, Apple has provided material for asteroid positions, and many other sources are making the information about Ceres, Pallas Athena, Juno and Vesta available to astrologers of all levels. Research is going forward with many of the other bodies in the asteroid belt as well. The more information which is readily available, the more people will be using these bodies in their natal and predictive horoscopes which will add greatly to the information about them.

If this series of books does no more than stimulate one other astrologer to investigate the asteroid belt it will have served its cosmic purpose.

Emma Belle Donath
Summer 1982

FOREWORD

Asteroids — should they play a significant role in astrology today? Different astrologers have various viewpoints regarding asteroids and are not quite sure how they should fit in OR even if they *should* fit in — and, so, why 4 for one sign? Some people swear by them; others feel perhaps it is no more important than a point on a chart, vertex, or arabian point, but seems to be an enigma among many astrologers. Of course, there is the "Titius-Bode Law" showing that the asteroids should be located at 2.8 astronomical units from the sun. That theory certainly pinpointed their location and roughly that of Saturn and Uranus but not beyond this point. However, when examining the prime number of formalism devised by Dr. Theodor Landscheidt, (an astronomer, mathematician, and physicist) we find:

Dr. Landschedit's later discovery shows there is a second generation of prime numbers consisting of the numbers 5, 7, 11 and 19. He applied these four numbers to Venus, Earth, Mars and the Planetoids. The second group of prime numbers is applied to Jupiter and Saturn. The third group is applied to Uranus, Neptune, and Pluto. The fourth is applied to Transpluto. In using the subshells of prime numbers, the number 7 is analogous to the first group; two 7's to the second group; three 14's to the third group; and four 42's to the fourth group. The relationship is as an electron is to a subshell of an atom compared with the periodic system of chemical elements as relates to planetary groups. With these individual classifications, the seven periods of elements can be developed.[1]

I	II	III	IV
-♀☿♂ Pl	♃ ♄	♆	Tp
7	7 7	14 14 14	42
1	2 3	4 5 6	7

Figure 1. Classification of Planetary Groups.

---

[1] John Robert Hawkins, M.S. *Transpluto or Should We Call Him BACCHUS The Ruler of Taurus?*, (Dallas, 1976), pp. 11-12.

The prime numbers as follows are assigned to each of the planets: Venus – 5; Earth – 7; Mars – 11; Planetoids – 19; Jupiter – 37; Saturn – 67; Uranus – 137; Neptune – 211; Pluto – 283; and Transpluto – 563. Earth is used as the astronomical unit one from the Sun. Divide 7 into, for example, the number for Mars. The result would be 1.5. Similarly, in dividing 7 (Earth) into 211 (Neptune) the result would be 30.1 — the approximate location of Neptune today in astronomical units. (Hawkins, 1976, pp. 11-12).

	♀	☿	♂	Pl	♃	♄		ψ		Tp
Titius–Bode	0,7	1	1,6	2,8	5,2	10	19,6	38,8	77,2	154
observed:	0,7	1	1,5	2,8	5,2	9,5	19,2	30,1	39,8*	(77-80)
number sequence:	0,7	1	1,5	2,7	5,2	9,5	19,3	29,9**	40,0	79,5

*Author's correction: 39,4   **Author's correction: 30,1

Figure 2. Planetary Distance (A.U.) by Prime Numbers.

Taking the sum of these prime numbers (1340) and applying the dimensionless number 1836.12 (the relationship between the masses of proton and electron) using the Fine Structure Constant (137.032), we find 1340 is the total of prime numbers since the precise ratio of the abstract number in physics collapses on the number of further rational numbers to the sum rn. The factor is 10^2.

Looking at this, we find the planets are located very close — clear out to Transpluto (Bacchus) where they should be today. This is very significant and further reading in Dr. Landscheidt's book, *Cosmic Cybernetics*, relates these different chemical periodical groups related to different planets. Thus, by "Titius-Bode Law" and Prime Number formalism at 2.8 A.U., a planetary body should be represented.

In mythology, it is also very significant when looking at the planets themselves, the different gods and goddesses, and how they apply in today's world. We find there are only certain planets named from a certain group of gods and goddesses. Mythology has given the key. Neptune rules the twelfth house (the sign of Pisces) which holds the secrets and the mysteries finding...

Greek mythology begins with Uranus (heaven) and Gaea (earth), the parents of the Titans — six brothers and six sisters. The Titans, incited by Gaea, overthrew Uranus and made Saturn

(Chronos), their younger brother, the ruler. Chronos married his sister, Rhea, and from this union came six major Greek Gods: Zeus, Hera, Hades, Poseidon, Demeter, and Hestia. Zeus, after dethroning Chronos, became the father of all the other great gods and goddesses — Athena, Apollo, Artemis, Ares, Hepaestus, Hermes, Dionysus and Aphrodite. All of these are in the Olympian group and all the planets in our solar system thus far named are from these gods and goddesses.

With the rise of Rome, the Greek names were replaced by Roman ones. Thus, Hestia became Vesta; Demeter, Ceres; Hera, Juno; Poseidon, Neptune, etc. Within this group, all the gods and goddesses have rulership power over certain signs of the zodaic. But, two signs remain unnamed — without a god or goddess. Uranus rules Aquarius; Saturn rules Capricorn; Neptune rules Pisces. Pluto was not named within this group because he was god of the underworld and thus was not on Mt. Olympus; however, he rules Scorpio. Jupiter rules Sagittarius; Hermes or Mercury rules Gemini; Apollo, the Sun, rules Leo; Artemis or Diana, the Moon, rules Cancer; Ares or Mars rules Aries; and Aphrodite or Venus rules Libra. Only two signs remain unnamed — Taurus and Virgo. The mythological meanings of Vesta, Ceres, Juno and Athena (for Minerva or Pallas) have to do more with Virgo (Hawkins, 1976, p. 16).

Firstly, there were two great Earth gods — one called Bacchus, known as both the wine and bull god, and the other Demeter (or Ceres) the goddess of corn or small grains.[2] Bacchus was also called Taurus, the bull god.[3] The constellation Virgo represents a woman with a branch in her right hand and some ears of corn in her left. The Hebrew name for Virgo is "a virgin". The constellation of Virgo itself describes her as a woman with ears of corn.[4] Further, this is stated — "the Terrestial Virgin Mother is Ceres, or Demeter, and Virgo is identified with her — Virgin Mother of World Saviors — Ceres, Myrrha, Mary — were inducted into the Virgin mysteries or Madonna Rites under the Virgo Hierarchy —".[5] This is what Ceres or Demeter, in Greek and Roman mythology was — the goddess of

[2] Edith Hamilton, *Mythology*, (New American Library, New York, 1969), p. 47.
[3] Robert Graves, *The Greek Myths: J*, (Penguin Books, Baltimore, Maryland, 1960), p. 296.
[4] Howard B. Rand, *The Stars Declare God's Handiwork*, (Merrimac, Mass., 1944), pp. 2-3.
[5] Corinne Heline, *Mythology and the Bible*, (New Age Press, Inc. La Canada, Calif., 1972), p. 23.

corn. Could anything be clearer than that the constellation itself assigns Ceres as goddess of Virgo!

Demeter (Ceres) was known as the great mother goddess, as known in the Eleusian mysteries which originated the virgin mother (virgin Mary) and the child theme. This was represented by the accompanying North Constellation of Virgo, known as Coma (woman and child). We find when her daughter, Kore or Persephone, was lost, or kidnapped by Pluto, she would not let any fruit or grain grow on Earth, causing famine until she recovered her daughter. She symbolizes what one really cares for or about. Pallas, the next significant goddess, was a goddess of understanding. She was very skilled in handicrafts and was called the mistress of industry. The ancient name for the accompanying constellation (Coma) of Virgo, meant desired or the longed for...the identical word for the Holy Spirit in Hag 2:7.[6] The Holy Spirit in the Bible is symbolized by olive oil and means light, understanding and wisdom. The parable of the ten virgins shows only five virgins were wise and had oil in their lamps. It is significant because Pallas was called the goddess of wisdom, also symbolized by the olive tree and represents analyzing the parts and putting them together to make a whole. Pallas is what you know and understand.

The first two asteroids are located and rotate at 2.767 A.U. and 4.6012 sidereal years; and 2.772 A.U. and 4.6069 sidereal years, respectively. Both are closest to the prime number formalism and the "Titius-Bode Law" and were the first two discovered of the asteroids. Ceres, the largest, was discovered New Year's Day, 1801, and Pallas, March 28, 1802. These two planetoids play a major role in the sign of Virgo. Then the planetoid Juno, wife of Jupiter, was discovered September 1, 1804, and Vesta, the vestal virgin, followed on March 29, 1807.

Another accompanying North constellation of Virgo is Bootes (the Coming One). In addition to the reaper pictured by the sickle it means to tread underfoot, anger and vengeance. (Rand, 1944, p. 3). Juno depicted this with her fits of jealousy, anger and vengeance she reaped on those involved with her husband Jupiter. Juno represents critical ability. Vesta, the vestal virgin, kept the fires and offered sacrifices of the fruits or harvest and meal offerings — these were sin offerings and in particular represented healing of the body. She was the purest of all (asteroid Vesta is the only asteroid unmarked and unpotted), and is represented by the other accompany-

---

[6] Rand, p.3

ing constellation South of Virgo, known as Asmeath, meaning sin-offering or making one's soul as an offering for sin. (Rand, 1944, p. 3). This is why Vesta represents a job or duty that is dull and boring to the point that it becomes a sacrifice. Vesta also equates to security; the constellation and accompanying constellations of Virgo itself tell its rulers by their meanings. What could be plainer than the constellation itself! God challenged Job: "Canst Thou bring forth the Mazzorth (the twelve signs of the Zodiac or constellations of the Zodiac) in his season?" Job 38:32. The Hebrews knew the original meanings of the constellations. This divine knowledge was preserved by them. Will one argue with the Maker of the Heavens?

It is very interesting that it took another 38 years before the next asteroid was discovered. Could it not be that the heavens themselves were telling us these four planetoids would play the major role in the asteroid belt — the four being virgins as represented by the name Virgo? No wonder, these were the only four goddesses left on Mt. Olympus. Why should there be four planetoids ruling the sign of Virgo and not just one? This is very intriguing to most. Let's examine: First, the concept of Virgo means to serve. If there were one rulership, one would be served, rather than serving — losing the complete meaning of Virgo. It is the mass (the working classes) serving the one big boss. Therefore, the rulership of Virgo must be made up of more than one ruler in Virgo. The working class of people are told what to do. That is why in the asteroid belt, the planets Mars and Jupiter influence the rotational movement of the asteroids, without complete freedom on their own, and to a certain degree are more or less told what to do, unlike planets which rule their own signs.

The next question is why the number four? The number four is a basic number. The Empedoclean concept is four elements: fire, air, water and earth. In Heitzenberg's universal formula, he is convinced that in all elementary processes, from which all natural phenomena evolve, four different groups are to be distinguished. Along with this we find that there are four classes of elementary particles, namely the photon group, the leptons,and mesons and the baryons. In addition, Dirac Friedemann, and Eddington endeavor to devise structural models comprehensively reflecting natural phenomena, all used four basic elements as a starting point.[7] Also, we find in the prime number formalism used there were four elements consisting

---

[7]Dr. Theodor Landscheidt, *Cosmic Cybernetics The Foundations of a Modern Astrology*, (Federal Republic of Germany, 1973), pp. 26-27.

of 5, 7, 11 and 19. It is extremely interesting because it is a foundation or a basis. Perhaps what is more interesting and important is the digestive system which Virgo represents.

Of the asteroids, Ceres is the largest and when asteroids get larger in number generally they get smaller in size. It is believed that there are up to 200,000 asteroids, and all of them have not yet been found. This is certainly indicative in defining Virgo when it comes to numbers and details as they get smaller and smaller, much like the digestive system and the way food is brought in (which is Ceres, the gatherer) and then is continually broken down until digested. Further in the digestive system, there are four major parts: first the mouth and saliva which brings in the large particles of food by being analyzed and critically examined as to where it should be broken down; the small intestine, where food is broken down and digested; and finally, the large intestine, the end result of what is pure and what is to be eliminated in waste. Notice that the large food particles are broken down smaller and smaller, the same as the asteroid belt. The stomach of a herbivorous animal has four parts that determine where different food particles should go. There are four enzymes in the digestive system — one breaks down proteins, one starches, one fats, and one sugars — four as a whole. It should be clear that there are four planetoids/asteroids which make up the sign of Virgo. Additionally, there are only four virgins left of the Olympian goddesses, all of which had mythological meanings pertaining to the sign of Virgo. Ceres, the goddess of grain and the great gatherer, had to do with the agricultural industry. Pallas, the mistress of industry, pertains to the non-agricultural industry. These two goddesses serve the two major industries. Juno, the wife of Jupiter who took her virginal rites yearly to remain a virgin, portrays serving in a marital state. Vesta, the vestal virgin, portrays serving in an unmarried state. Service is the real meaning behind Virgo.

Examining the different services each asteroid provides, one learns in detail how service is to really be performed. It is no small wonder Christ got angry at some of his disciples when they were trying to determine who would sit on His right hand. Then, Christ said — "let him that would be the greatest among you be the servant of all—". In other words, the greatest master is the greatest servant of all, or he who serves the most. This is what Virgo teaches in great detail.

How significant are the asteroids within one's chart? Looking at the asteroids, we deal with details and finer points within a chart, naturally. Some people say this is a lot of work. This is true because that is exactly what Virgo represents — a lot of work and a lot of service. If you are going to get down to real details in a chart, then you bring these in. It is obvious the four asteroids have a great deal of power even though their relative size is small. One realizes that the power of planets come not from size or distance from the sun, but by its material content as witnessed by Pluto, small in size and yet farthest from the sun.

In the past there has been a significant amount of work done regarding asteroids, both by Eleanor Bach and Zipporah Pottenger Dobyns, PhD., but no one until now has put it all together. Now, Emma Belle Donath has done just that. We have not only an ephemeris, but the planets in signs, in houses, aspects to each other, and midpoints. This is a major undertaking to be completed on any subject in astrology, let along the sign of Virgo. This series goes a long way to answer many questions. Naturally continual research needs to be done to keep the material updated. This series of books, however, is a major foundation on which to build future knowledge.

John Robert Hawkins, M.S.

BIBLIOGRAPHY

Graves, Robert. *The Greek Myths: F*, Penguin Books, Baltimore, Maryland, 1960

Hamilton, Edith. *Mythology*, New American Library, New York, NY, 1969

Hawkins, John Robert, M.S. *Transpluto or Should We Call Him BACCHUS The Ruler of Taurus?*, Hawkins Enterprising Publications, Dallas, Texas, 1976

Heline, Corinne. *Mythology and the Bible*, New Age Press, Inc., La Canada, Calif., 1972

Landscheidt, Theodore, Dr. *Cosmic Cybernetics*, Ebertin-Verlag, D-7080 Aalen/Wurtt., Federal Republic of Germany, 1973

Rand, Howard B. *The Stars Declare God's Handiwork*, Destiny Publishers, Merrimac, Mass., 1944.

This foreword entitled "Why Should the Asteroids Rule the Sign of Virgo?" was reproduced with permission from copyrighted material from John Robert Hawkins.

Chapter 1.

ASTROLOGICAL SYSTEMS AND RULERSHIPS

Mankind senses the greater and lesser cycles about him whether called astrology or not. He or she is aware of the rising and setting of the Sun each day replaced by the Moon at night. Other time periods are related to various planetary energies orbiting at different rates. Volumes have been written speculating about actual origins of the twin sciences of astronomy and astrology. The prevalent concepts follow the Greek school of study, often called Ptolemaic, established around 150 to 200 A.D. This system, and others, are presumably based on more ancient investigations from Egypt, Babylon, Chaldea and possibly even fabled Atlantis. Other disciplines follow the eastern traditions of China and India. Three types of compatible systems were used in the research of this book: an updated version of the Ptolemaic zodiac positions and aspects, planetary pictures plus transneptunian energies of the Hamburg School of Astrology, and midpoints of the cosmobiologists. All of these systems were most frequently considered with the planets positioned in the tropical zodiac. Since angles between planets, or aspects, would not be changed by transfer to sidereal positions, the delineations may be used by advocates of both systems. Only sign and house rulership suggestions, discussed in this chapter, would necessarily be modified for use with the constellations.

PTOLEMAIC ASPECTS AND RULERSHIPS

The term *aspect* is used to define any mathematical angle between two planets. More easily calculated aspects, degrees divisible by 30, are called *major aspects* and include the sextile or 60 degree angle, the square or 90 degree angle, the trine or 120 degree angle, the quincunx or 150 degrees, the opposition or 180 degrees and the conjunction or zero degrees apart. Other aspects are clumped into harmonic relationships, all divisible by a common factor such as 45 degrees. These so-called *hard-aspects* include semi-square or 45 degree angles, square or 90 degrees, sesqui-quadrate or 135 degrees, and opposition or 180 degrees. Some schools further divide these angles into 22-1/2, 11-1/4 and 5-5/8 degree angles.

Another category being investigated includes aspects divided by 18 degrees making the vigintile, decile, quintile, square, tredecile and biquintile. This investigation was originated by Kepler. The 360-degree circle can be divided by any number to form aspects. Pioneering work in this field has been done by the late John Addey whose research is now classified under the heading of *Harmonics*.

Whether the faster-moving planet is traveling away from or toward the slower-moving body is also relevant in discussing aspects. When Mars, for example, is moving away from a recent conjunction with the Sun it is termed separating. If, however, Mars has gone past 180 degrees, or half the zodiac circle, since its conjunction with the Sun then it is approaching or returning to a new conjunction with the Sun. This can either be expressed by giving the exact degree difference between conjunction and present position or by adding clarifying statements with the aspect name. Table 1 presents aspects in exact degrees along with commonly used glyphs or symbols.

Aspect	Degrees	Waxing or Separating	Degree	Waning or Approaching
Conjunction	0	Unity	360	New Beginnings
Vigintile	18	Launching	342	Culmination
Semi-Oktil	22-1/2	Speed Up	337-1/2	Slow Down
Quindecile	24	Momentum	336	Braking
Semi-Sextile	30	Emergence	330	Integration
Decile	36	Resources	324	Support
Novile	40	Development	320	Nurturing
Semi-Square	45	Upsets	315	Stresses
Septile	51-3/7	Focusing	308-4/7	Commitment
Sextile	60	Opportunity	300	Application
Quintile	72	Insight	288	Talent/Transformation
Square	90	Major Crisis	270	Tests
Biseptile	102-6/7	Zeal	257-1/7	Dedication
Tredecile	108	Cornerstone	252	Unfoldment
Trine	120	Expansion	240	Blending/Absorption
Sesqui-Quadrate	135	Difficulties	225	Agitation
Biquintile	144	Advantage	216	Perception
Quincunx	150	Dilemma	210	Revision
Triseptile	154-2/7	Collective Need Considered	205-5/7	Cooperation
Opposition	180	Encounter	180	Repolarization

Table 1. Astrological aspect keywords.

In traditional astrology, planetary energies react according to their mathematical relationship or aspect. Thus, the aspect keyword becomes the verb or acting word between two subjects or nouns. Delineations given in Chapter 3 show planetary energies at the top of each page to be used when only two planets are considered. For example, Pallas Athena/Venus equals whichever of the following interpretations is appropriate:

Pallas Athena semi-square Venus = Career stresses for women.
Pallas Athena semi-sextile Venus = Professional opportunities for a female worker.
Pallas Athena square Venus = Crisis incurred by a woman's job.
Pallas Athena trine Venus = Girl's promotion in school or profession.
Pallas Athena quincunx Venus = Working schedule demands revision of female dress code.
Pallas Athena opposition Venus = Conflicts from woman's co-workers.

Many times there are more than two planets reacting together natally, by transit or by progression. Such familiar configurations as grand trine, grand cross, T-square and yod are really midpoint structures. For example, Pallas Athena at 12 Cancer trine Jupiter at 12 Scorpio trine Saturn at 12 Pisces may just as accurately be expressed as Jupiter/Saturn equals Pallas Athena, Pallas Athena/Saturn equals Jupiter, or Pallas Athena/Jupiter equals Saturn.

A T-square of the Moon at 5 Gemini square Neptune at 5 Virgo and Vesta at 5 Pisces could only be written as Vesta/Neptune equals Moon. A yod of Sun at 17 Aries sextile Juno at 17 Gemini both quincunx Mars at 17 Scorpio would be shown only as Sun/Juno equals Mars. Midpoints are not limited to the major aspect degrees.

Rulerships for mundane, horary or electional horoscopes are often limited to the Ptolemaic or ancient concepts of the double ladder of planetary rulerships using only the seven first visible planets, as shown in Table 2.

Most natal or personal astrological charts today are delineated by adding the outer planets in the relationship pattern shown in Table 3.

Asteroid interpretations for sign and house position are presented in detail in *Asteroids in the Birth Chart*, by Donath. Delineations for other planets in house and sign position are presented at length in numerous texts. There seems to be no need, therefore, to duplicate that effort in this particular book.

3

House	Sign	Ruling Planets	Glyph
1	Aries	Mars	♂
2	Taurus	Venus	♀
3	Gemini	Mercury	☿
4	Cancer	Moon	☽
5	Leo	Sun	☉
6	Virgo	Mercury	☿
7	Libra	Venus	♀
8	Scorpio	Mars	♂
9	Sagittarius	Jupiter	♃
10	Capricorn	Saturn	♄
11	Aquarius	Saturn	♄
12	Pisces	Jupiter	♃

Table 2.   Old system of planetary rulerships.

House	Sign	Ruling Planets	Glyph
1	Aries	Mars	♂
2	Taurus	Venus or Transpluto	♀ ⚴
3	Gemini	Mercury	☿
4	Cancer	Moon	☽
5	Leo	Sun	☉
6	Virgo	Mercury or Asteroid Belt	☿ ⚵
7	Libra	Venus or Transpluto	♀ ⚴
8	Scorpio	Pluto or Mars	♇ ♂
9	Sagittarius	Jupiter	♃
10	Capricorn	Saturn	♄
11	Aquarius	Uranus	♅
12	Pisces	Neptune	♆

Table 3.   Current system of planetary rulerships.

URANIAN ASTROLOGY CONCEPTS

During the early decades of this century an outer belt of small planets (or asteroids) was found to have effects in the horoscope. Most of this work was done by the German astrologer Alfred Witte and his students. These followers of Herr Witte researched new concepts of midpointing and sensitive points outside the known planetary energy fields. Witte himself only lived to see four of these transneptunian planets used. Others tested out four more bodies, developing placements and keywords, to be used in the so-called Hamburg, Germany, School of Astrology widely known now as Uranian Astrology. Astronomers and some astrologers negate the possibility of any of these transneptunian bodies because the work did not include Pluto, which was discovered in the 1930's.

Whether the transneptunian planets, Pluto and even Transpluto are individual planets, or actually an outer asteroid belt, is open to investigation and conjecture. There are similarities with the inner asteroid belt, such as their two and one-half to seven and one-half year orbits compared with the 250-year and 750-year orbital periods of the outer transneptunians. General positions in both cases correlate with a placement of a planet suggested by both Bode and Titius. Vulcanus and Transpluto fit most closely the space designated mathematically for the next outer planet to be located. Figures for the distances from the Sun and the periods of revolution for the transneptunian planets vary among different authors of Uranian texts. Data are given in Table 4 from the work done by Witte and Friedrich Sieggrun as translated by Udo Rudolph in *The Hamburg School of Astrology, An Explanation of Its Methods.* Transpluto data are from the text on that planet by John Robert Hawkins presented according to the calculations by astronomer Emil Sevin, updated and precession corrected by Hawkins.

Traditional planetary data are those presently used by the astrological community from current periodicals. Speculations about Vulcan will be discussed in the chapter on planetary energies. Keywords for the various planetary bodies are given in Table 5.

In the Uranian School of Astrology certain points within the horoscope are found to link the native to planetary positions of the day. These are termed *personal points.* Any aspect or planetary picture lacking a personal point tie is unimportant for that native. Traditional personal points include the Midheaven, Ascendant, Aries Point or zero degree of any cardinal sign, Moon's North Node,. the Sun and the Moon. Some astrologers are now including the Vertex and Lilith as additional personal points. These energy points are calculated in the same manner as for traditional astrology, as shown by the forms in Appendix A.

Planetary pictures are simply the use of planets posited at varying distances from a common point. When two planets are equally distant from a third planet they are called midpoints. For

Glyph	Planet	A.U.	Period of Revolution
☿	Vulcan	0.177	19 days
☿	Mercury	0.387	88 days
♀	Venus	0.723	224.7 days
⊕	Earth	1.000	365.25 days
♂	Mars	1.524	687 days
⚳	Ceres	2.767	4.6 years
♃	Jupiter	5.203	11.86 years
♄	Saturn	9.539	29.18 years
♅	Uranus	19.18	84.01 years
♆	Neptune	30.06	164.8 years
♇	Pluto	39.41	247.7 years
⚴	Cupido	42.1	262 years
⊕	Hades	50.6	360 years
⚵	Zeus	57.3	455 years
⚶	Kronos	62.4	521 years
⚷	Apollon	68.9	576 years
⚸	Admetos	71.5	624 years
⚹	Transpluto	77.8	656-685 years
⚺	Vulcanus	78.7	663 years
♓	Poseidon	82.8	740 years

**Table 4.   Our solar system. One A.U. equals the
distance from the Earth to the Sun.**

example, Mars at 29 Aries trine Moon at 29 Sagittarius would have
a midpoint of 29 Aquarius. On a day when Pallas Athena was transit-
ing 29 Aquarius a new job contract was offered and accepted by a
person whose Ascendant was also aspected. The structure would be
written thus:

$$Moon/Mars = Pallas\ Athena_T$$

Other sensitive points react when planets form mathematical
equations by addition or subtraction of other planets. Thus, planets
may be substituted for letters in the following equations:

$$x + y = z + w \text{ which may also be written as}$$
$$x + y - z = w$$

Various combinations of this formula are found in the use of
planetary pictures so long as the sum of each side remains equal to
the sum of the other side. This system is more fully explained in
textbooks devoted entirely to the study of Uranian Astrology.

Glyph	Planet or Personal Point	Keyword
M	Midheaven	I or "Ich"
A	Ascendant	You or "Du"
Vx	Vertex	Responses, Release
♈	Aries Point	World in General
☊	Nodes	Connections
☉	Sun	Physical body
☽	Moon	Emotional body
⊘	Lilith	Willingness to Succumb
♉	Vulcan	Isolate/Urge to Free
☿	Mercury	Think/Talk
♀	Venus	Comfort/Want
⊕	Earth	Support/Form
♂	Mars	Work/Energy
⚳	Ceres	Nurture
⚴	Pallas Athena	Organize/Conserve
⚵	Juno	Structure
⚶	Vesta	Dedicate/Fire
♃	Jupiter	Grow/Protect
♄	Saturn	Teach/Delegate
♅	Uranus	Excite/Innovate
♆	Neptune	Veil/Dissolve
♇	Pluto	Alter/Change
⚴	Cupido	Expand/Adhere
⊕	Hades	Clean Up/Disintegrate
⚵	Zeus	Project/Aim
⚶	Kronos	Elevate/Lead
♃	Apollon	Multiply/Specialize
♄	Admetos	Delay/Steady
⚶	Vulcanus	Force/Overpower
♓	Poseidon	Enlighten/Illuminate
⚶	Bacchus/Transpluto	Shock/Transform

Table 5.   Planetary energy keywords.

The Hamburg School prefers the Libra rising or Earth chart with an equal division of the houses for the basic relationship of the native to his general surroundings. Basic meanings for each house remain the same as in the traditional system. However, the rulership affinities differ, as shown in Table 6.

House	Sign	Ruling Planets	Glyph
1	Libra	Cupido	⚷
2	Scorpio	Neptune + Pluto	♆ + ♇
3	Sagittarius	Uranus	♅
4	Capricorn	Saturn	♄
5	Aquarius	Jupiter	♃
6	Pisces	Poseidon + Asteroids	⚳ + ⚴
7	Aries	Mars + Vulcanus	♂ + ⚴
8	Taurus	Earth + Admetos	⊕ + ⚴
9	Gemini	Venus + Apollon	♀ + ⚴
10	Cancer	Mercury + Kronos	☿ + ⚴
11	Leo	Zeus	⚴
12	Virgo	Hades	⚴

Table 6.   One system of rulerships in Uranian Astrology.

Rather than any consideration of planets in signs, the degree position of a planet defines its position on the 360 or 90 degree dial, as explained in Appendix B. Sometimes the planet is used as if it were conjunct the sign ruler. For example, if the following condition were found — Sun in Capricorn square Moon in Libra — it would be written as Sun plus Saturn equals Moon plus Cupido. Or Juno in Aquarius sesqui-quadrate Venus in Virgo would be expressed as Juno plus Jupiter equals Venus plus Hades. This applies only in natal delineation, not in the adding of sums or half-sums. Planets are not considered as rulers of particular house cusps in the German techniques.

COSMOBIOLOGY CONCEPTS

Principle factors involved in the study of cosmobiology are the cosmogram, halfsums or midpoints, cosmic structure patterns, graphic ephemerides, solar arc directions and the term *stellar bodies* rather than planets. Reinhold Ebertin, Dr. Baldur Ebertin and Dr. Walter Koch lead the list of famous scientists who have spent many years researching the relationship between mankind and stellar motion, using the 90-degree dial and midpoint system of cosmobiology.

In looking at a cosmogram the planetary positions are shown both in a 360-degree and a 90-degree dial for visual convenience as seen in Figure 3. Meanings of the stellar or planetary energies are given as primary principles, psychological correspondences, biological correspondences, sociological correspondences and delineations in direct and indirect midpoints rather than being discussed in relation to houses, signs and aspects. Although explanations are given in the subject material for the various astrological houses, no house system is used in cosmobiology.

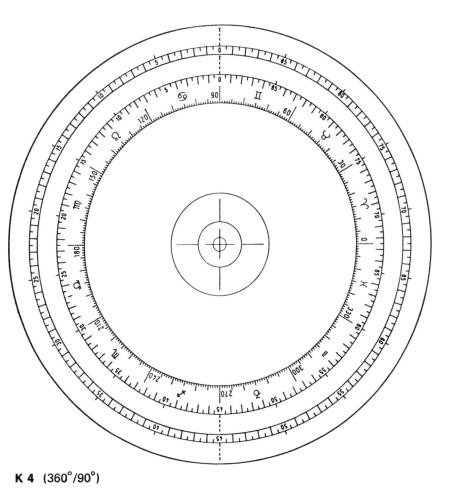

K 4 (360°/90°)

Figure 3. An Example Cosmogram.

9

Much significant medical research has been done in the field of cosmobiology and physical correspondences are discussed, as well as other factors, in *The Combination of Stellar Influences*, by Ebertin. Similar material for Transpluto is given by John Hawkins in his text on that outer planet.

THEORIES OF ESOTERIC ASTROLOGY

Esoteric astrology deals with further understanding of human subjectivity, or soul, rather than events and personality. Emphasis is on relationship of the individual anima-animus. Flow of planetary energies through various human bodies indicates inner reaction and response to outer activity.

Devotees of this branch of astrology write that the intuitional approach is "bringing about a return to the knowledge of this ancient science related to the constellations and our solar system."[8] Aspects are considered to have basically the same meanings as in the traditional schools of thought. However, accepted planetary rulership patterns are changed considerably in esoteric exploration as shown in Table 7.

Yet another set of planet-sign affiliations are considered for those persons who are deemed disciples or adepts of their chosen

House	Sign	Ruling Planets	Glyph
1	Aries	Mercury	☿
2	Taurus	Vulcan	☊☿
3	Gemini	Venus	♀
4	Cancer	Neptune	♆
5	Leo	Sun[9]	☉
6	Virgo	Moon[9]	☽
7	Libra	Uranus	♅
8	Scorpio	Mars	♂
9	Sagittarius	Earth	⊕
10	Capricorn	Saturn	♄
11	Aquarius	Jupiter	♃
12	Pisces	Pluto	♀

Table 7.   Esoteric system of rulerships according to Alice Bailey.

[8] Alice Bailey, *Esoteric Astrology*, (Lucis Trust, New York, 1951), p. 3.
[9] Both the Sun and the Moon are said to veil other planets.

discipline. This is called the hierarchical pattern of relationships given in Table 8.

House	Sign	Ruling Planets	Glyph
1	Aries	Uranus	♅
2	Taurus	Vulcan	⛢
3	Gemini	Earth	⊕
4	Cancer	Neptune	♆
5	Leo	Sun[10]	☉
6	Virgo	Jupiter	♃
7	Libra	Saturn	♄
8	Scorpio	Mercury	☿
9	Sagittarius	Mars	♂
10	Capricorn	Venus	♀
11	Aquarius	Moon[10]	☽
12	Pisces	Pluto	♇

Table 8. Hierarchical system of rulerships according to Alice Bailey.

There remains considerable controversy among astrologers about whether the esoteric literature refers to rulership of tropical zodiac signs or sidereal affinity with the actual constellations. Early writers such as Alice Bailey and Madame Helena Blavatsky were not technically trained astrologers or astronomers and so used the terms sign and constellation interchangeably.

---

[10] Both the Sun and the Moon are said to veil other planets.

Chapter 2.
PLANETARY ENERGIES

A good study for understanding planetary energies is the reading of ancient myths or fairy tales about legendary gods or goddesses for whom the celestial bodies were named. The appropriate naming of planets seems to fit into a larger cosmic scheme which cannot be explained logically. In this chapter basic mythology is blended with current interpretations of the planets or luminaries being discussed.

Another valuable source of information about planets, or other heavenly bodies, is traditional and current astronomical information. No physical body will give off etheric energies which are contrary to its basic structure and activity. Because recent space probes and interplanetary flights have brought back new information about the planets in this solar system, it is wise for astrologers to be aware of recent discoveries.

No chapter on the planets can possibly cover all the plausible keywords or attributes of any given body so the following material is limited to a basic understanding of the celestial bodies presented.

VULCAN

This god of the forge was lamed after a fall from the heights of Mt. Olympus. Son of Jupiter and Juno, he was raised by mortals and later reinstated among the heavenly hosts. An expert artisan, Vulcan fashioned thunderbolts for Jupiter, designed gold sandals for the flying gods, made beautiful jewelry for the goddesses as well as forged weapons and armor for the warlike males. This deity was first married to unfaithful Venus and later more suitably matched with Charis, also called Grace. Some legends tell that Vulcan went out of the heavens as Pluto came in, others say he was replaced by Bacchus. Vulcan once made sport of his brother, Mars, before the council of gods and was ever after shunned by Mars. The hammer is symbolic of Vulcan's power to pound base metals into items of beauty or to free the chains of the slave. The author uses Vulcan positions and orbital times published by Carl Stahl. Individual midpoint structures are not given for this little-used body in the chapter on delineations but interested researchers may benefit from the information presented in the following keyword list.

Glyph: ♀ (with line above)

Keywords for Vulcan:

affliction overcome	emotes inwardly	metallurgist	silent suffering
artisan	exiles	muscular	stunning blow
battery	forges ahead	originator	tone deafness
behind scenes	fundamental	overshadowed	unappreciated
burns away dross	heartbroken	persistent	weakness eliminated
clarifies (as butter	homely	propman	withering
in cooking)	industrious	refines	worker
disciplines	lame	rehabilitated	wounded
discriminates	loveless	scarred	yearn

MERCURY

Mercury was messenger of the gods, lord of divine books, lord of divine word, god of letters, science, mathematics and wisdom; as well as being carrier of the serpent or kundalini fire. This son of Jupiter and Maia was known as Hermes to the Egyptians and Greeks, Wotan to the Germans, Nebo in Chaldea and Buddha to the Indians. During early childhood Mercury was in constant motion bringing new ideas where his feet touched Earth. Ever youthful, he continued to translate the rules and commands of the gods into words and symbols which mortal man could understand.

Glyph: ☿

Keywords for Mercury:

abstracts	bronchial tubes	impulsive	speaks
adapts	businessman	journalism	teachers
agility	catalyst	joy	telephones
alert	cerebrospinal nerves	limbs	thyroid
analysis	charming	lower mind	tongue
aware	communicates	mischievous	transmission
biases	comprehension	moves	twinning
books	debates	nervous	vocal cords
breath	dexterity	pickpockets	writing

VENUS

The question in dealing with this planetary energy is whether it really is Venus or Aphrodite. Venus was first the wife of Vulcan, then mistress of Mars, mother to Cupid, consort to her husband's brother, daughter of Jupiter and Dione, and finally chosen by mortal Paris as the fairest goddess on the mountain. The golden girdle of Venus gave such an air of beauty, grace and elegance that all who came near fell in adoration at her feet. Plato gave to this goddess the title of Venus Popularia and called the older, more mysterious goddess, Venus Urania, because she was reported to have sprung from the froth of the sea where Uranus's mutilated genitals were tossed. The parentless goddess Aphrodite better exemplifies the esoteric lord of the higher mind, or goddess of beauty and light, than the more popular Venus. Romans and Hebrews called this planet Lucifer during the periods of the year when it rose as the morning star.

Glyph: ♀

Keywords for Venus:

abstract thought	charm	furs	refinement
adroit	color	incense	sentiment
affection	decorations	jewelry	sister
appetites	dishevelment	luxuries	sloth
appreciation	dove	ovaries	sympathy
artistic	estrogen	parathyroid	taste
beauty	fatty tissue	peace	veins
cellulose	flirtations	pleasure	women

EARTH OR TERRA

Gaea was the old mother of all, including the sky represented by her son-husband Uranus, with whom she united to populate the heavens, ocean and earth. Other names of this goddess include Roman Tallus, Indian Tara, Egyptian Isis or Nat, Greek Ge, Te or Terra. Earth is the sure foundation or the solid base. Positioned exactly opposite the Sun, many of the attributes of the Sun are really reactions of Earth in the horoscope. Terra Firma is concerned with the place where man can experience reactions and relationships.

Glyph: ⊕

Keywords for Earth or Terra:

alive	courage	fulcrum point	reflective
apply	duality	healing	restorative
aqua color	evolving	interdependence	seasonal
balance	dense	intense	supportive
benign	diffusion	maternal	sustaining
compromise	fertile	possessive	womb

MARS

Son of Jupiter and Juno, this deity was brother to both Vulcan and Hebe, lover of Venus, god of war and husbandry, with the duty to dispel terror and fear. Mars has always been depicted as handsome but vain, being every ready to rush into battle. Bloodshed and

15

weaponry were common symbols of Mars whose other names include Greek Ares, Scandinavian Froh, Christian St. George, Chaldean Nergal, and Babylonian god of war and pestilence. In earlier days, Mars also portrayed the wise farmer who culled his flocks and grains in order to improve his acreage. This deity was concerned with providing for and protecting his family and village.

Glyph: ♂

Keywords for Mars:

action	challenge	hasten	nose
adventure	chivalry	honor	policeman
adrenaline	drive	injury	red
anger	energy	iron	survival
ardent	fever	knife	tools
athletics	force	lover	virility
brother	gall bladder	martial	will power
bestiality	gymnastics	mechanization	work

CERES OR DEMETER

This goddess was a daughter of Saturn and Rhea, sister of Zeus, Pluto, Poseidon, Vesta and Juno. She was concerned with planting seeds as well as being the goddess of harvest, deity of underground caves and springs, and the one who wielded the offering knife. Ceres was known to the Celts as Danna. Here is another of the mothering principles, devoid of emotionalism.

Glyph: ⚳

Keyword for Ceres:

adoption	digestion	instinct	pigs
ant	draperies	intestines (upper)	practical
antiseptic	ecology	habits	protective
austerity	fairs	harvest	salutary laws
bread	farm	laxatives	scythe
cereal	folded clothes	laundry	springs
civilizing	harvest	menses	toilet
clothes chest	honey	nurse	warts
domesticate	hospitals	nurture	wounds

PALLAS ATHENA

Athens was named for the benefactress who gave the olive tree to Greece. Pallas Athena, goddess of wisdom, was fully dressed and armed when thrust from her father's brow. This daughter of Zeus and Themis (whom Zeus swallowed) was also known as the goddess of cities and defense. Pallas trains the energy which Mars so abundantly owns. This goddess was known as a great breaker and tamer of horses which the warriors rode into battle.

Glyph: ♀

Keywords for Pallas Athena:

allocate	earnest	liaison	shield
armour	crusader	library	skills
bartering	employment	mathematics	trigger
beetle	flute	noble	uniforms
bravery	guardian	owl	valiant
conservation	handcrafts	pattern	vocation
counsel	independent	sculptor	wisdom
cunning	iris	spinning	women's rights

JUNO

Rightful wife of Jupiter, Juno was also sister to this king of the gods, through their shared parentage of Saturn and Rhea. Juno was known as goddess of maternity and marriage, concerned with childbirth, matrons and ceremonies. Keeper of the mint, the only married goddess on Mt. Olympus, Juno was frustrated by her lack of actual power. Juno, or Greek Hera, was a beautiful but jealous wife who spent much of her time and energy restoring her youthful charms.

Glyph: ⚵

Keywords for Juno:

bee	eccentric	migraine	salves
birth (happy)	eggs	nosey	sceptre
bossy	etiquette	ornamentation	shrewd
bride	fidelity	protocol	subtle
coiffure	host/hostess	parties	treasurer
contraceptives	jeweled	perpetuating	uptight
co-ruler	keys	pharmacist	vindictive
cosmetics	lilies	reflected glory	wiles
documents	marriage	restrictive	yoke

VESTA

As the eldest daughter of Saturn and Rhea, the goddess Vesta, or Hestia, was sister to reigning Jupiter. She remained a virgin and was considered as a goddess of the sacred fires of the temple and hearth. In Greece this deity was called Hestia. Vestal virgins of the various temple services were named for this model of devotion and served their gods for set periods of time, after which they were free to wed and bear children.

17

Glyph: ⍦
Keywords for Vesta:

acolyte	cultural heritage	hearth	spider
altar	dedicated	kiln fired	stability
archives	deer	laurel	traditions
candles	fanatic	masks	tripod
ceramics	geneology	periods of servitude	warmth
cleansing	graves	sanctuary	zealous

JUPITER

This youngest son of Saturn and Rhea released his brothers who had been swallowed up by their father at birth. He perpetuated the policy begun by his father when Saturn castrated his own father, Uranus. Jupiter, or Greek Zeus, ruled on Mt. Olympus along with his siblings plus the children of his many matings. In dividing the universe, brother Pluto took the underworld with its myriad actions, Neptune ruled the sea with it affinity to man's emotional life, leaving Jupiter to the earth and the sky along with the attributes of thought and wisdom. Some of Jupiter's other titles are Christian St. Peter, Pantheon Marduk and Hindu Brahmanaspati.

Glyph: ♃
Keywords for Jupiter:

abundance	ethics	joviality	priest
arteries	excess	judge	publishing
benevolence	expand	liver	seer
bigotry	favoritism	magnetic	status
blood plasma	fortune	massive	thunderbolt
civil servant	funeral	middle age	turbulence
culture	gall secretion	philosophy	turquoise
ennobling	influential	pituitary gland	universality

SATURN

This son of Uranus and Gaea castrated his father, thus taking the life-giving force from Uranus. Adult Saturn became father to Jupiter and most of the other inhabitants of Mt. Olympus, following his period as ruler of the universe during the Golden Age. The deity Saturn has long been called the lord of karma, the dweller on the threshold, the throat chakra of the solar logos, a true husband and Old Father Time. Saturn was eventually punished for not sharing the earth's bounty with his children and his monstrous Cyclops brothers.

18

Glyph: ♄

Keywords for Saturn:

administrator	concentration	hearing	schedules
aging	contraction	nest	serious
alienation	dentistry	orders	severe
authority	discipline	organizes	skeleton
banishment	examinations	parental	skin
bone	fences	pessimism	stones
character	form	guilt	teeth
coldness	grades	restrictions	trials

URANUS

Oldest of the known gods, Uranus married Gaea and bred many children including the Cyclops, the Titans and various monsters. Uranus was then mutilated by his son, Saturn, who took over rulership of the heavens and the earth. Uranus was originally thought of as the sky who married the earth and he shows enlarged dimensions of life, such as power above the normal range.

Glyph: ♅

Keywords for Uranus:

aloofness	dynamic	maverick	reform
authoritative	electric	modification	ruptures
autonomic nerves	engineers	mutation	spasmodic
capricious	experiments	nervous energy	uncharted
circulation	freedom	occult	unusual
conductivity	gadgets	oscillations	uranium
curious	impulsive	polarization	vibrations
durable	insight	professional	willful

NEPTUNE

As brother of Pluto and Jupiter as well as a son of Saturn and Rhea, Neptune was a moody and violent god who raced over the waves in a chariot drawn by a team of white horses. Neptune ruled the oceans, which entitled him to create earthquakes at his caprice. This god of the waters eventually became second in command, answerable only to his brother Jupiter.

Glyph: ♆

Keywords for Neptune:

addict	chemists	filters	mirages
alcohol	coma	fish	mystery
amnesia	curiosity	fluids	paralysis
aura	dreams	gas	odors
body tissues	electromagnetic	hypnotic	radiation
camouflage	enchantment	inspires	sailor
chaotic	enzymes	intrigue	spy
compassion	fantasy	lyden glands	trance

19

PLUTO

The gods forged a cloak of invisibility for Pluto which allowed him to capture his victims without being seen by them. Then the captured ones were taken to Pluto's underground kingdom. For this son of Saturn and Rhea ruled the underground and action, leaving the earth and sky to brother Jupiter. Pluto once stole pretty, young Persephone from her mother Ceres, and caused such chaos that the growing seasons of the earth were disturbed for a whole year.

Glyph: ♇

Keywords for Pluto:

analyst	fanaticism	plumbers	toxin
atomic fusion	gangster	regeneration	transform
blackmail	invisible changes	reproductive	tyranny
body pH	masses	revelation	unfoldment
cataclysm	meditation	sex appetites	upheaval
excretions	metamophosis	subconscious	urethra
detective	neurosis	surgeon	underworld
faddish	perineum	swaying	victims

TRANSPLUTO OR BACCHUS

Bacchus was the legendary god of wine ruling lavishly over feasts and festivals, sharing merriment with all who joined him. This god represents, on the other hand, the communion wine of the resurrection. John Robert Hawkins has written a comprehensive book on this as-yet-undiscovered planet, entitled *Transpluto or Shall We Call Him Bacchus, Ruler of Taurus?*, which includes keywords and midpoint correspondences.

CUPIDO

This son of Venus and Mercury fell in love with a mortal named Psyche. Cupido was usually seen as a chubby, naked little boy bearing golden wings; and representing joy to all. In addition, Cupido coordinated the elements of the universe, bringing harmony to chaos and permitting life to develop. Cupido is the ultimate theme of love and lovers, the consummation of marriage between congenial parties. He represents pleasurable unions of all types.

Glyph: ♃
Keywords for Cupido:

associations	corporation	joyfulness	success
belonging	creative	marriage	summary
camaraderie	expanding	merger	strings
clannishness	family	organizations	synthesis
cliques	gathering	participation	together
clubs	hereditary factors	romance	united
community	internal organ	schools	whole
coordinator	joint endeavors	society	winged

HADES

Hades is another name for Pluto and seems to include the underworld connotation plus the energies of the Moon, Saturn and Neptune in combination. This planet represents a bridge between physical and metaphysical worlds. Pluto overcomes death while Hades decays or shows the necessity for purification. Hades breaks down the whole into its component parts for analysis or cleansing. This planet is prominent in the charts of social workers and psychiatrists who work with people to bring basic changes in their lives.

Glyph: ♆
Keywords for Hades:

abnormal	buried treasure	dirt	mint herb
aggravation	compost	doctors	moles
antiques	corpse	fertilizer	orphans
archaeology	crime	ghetto	quicksand
ashes	cypress	history	scavengers
astrology	decomposition	impoverished	swamps
bacteria	defect	junk	vulgar
base	derelict	intestines	waste
bogs	disorder	manure	worms

ZEUS

Another name for Jupiter, this youngest son of Saturn and Rhea became king of the heavens through force and determination. Zeus is also called Hercules by some astrologers. This planet stands for working with a goal or an aim, carefully planned activity, creativity directed toward a purpose and focusing. The Cyclops fashioned thunderbolts for Zeus to throw against his adversaries.

When correctly aimed, these fiery arrows were as deadly as a modern missile.

Glyph: ⚡

Keywords for Zeus:

achieving	egotism	machinery	railroads
ambition	explosives	mechanics	reckless
application	fiery	military	rockets
armed forces	focused	missiles	thrust
cannons	force	overconfident	thunderbolts
command material	fuels	procreation	timed efforts
creation	gunfire	power tools	weapons of war
deliberate	initiative	purposeful	wise leaders

KRONOS

Wanting to always be in charge of all he was around created problems for this god whose other name is Saturn. Kronos refused to share rulership of the universe with either his siblings or his children, for which he was eventually dethroned. While Kronos ruled, there was absolute monarchy with all the grandeur and nobility associated. Kronos alone determined the proper time for actions like a large, universal clock.

Glyph: ♄

Keywords for Kronos:

authority	domineering	governor	maturity
bureaucracy	elevated	high merit	prestige
captain	elite	juror	red tape
celebrity	eminence	king	rules
chief	father	law	superiority
control	godfather	mastery	witness

APOLLON

Apollon, or Apollo, was the master musician of the gods and goddesses. As son of Leto and Jupiter, this deity was also twin brother of Artemis. Apollo was sometimes used as another name for the Sun. The god of light, purity and truth, Apollo revealed the future through his oracle at Delphi. Apollo was also skilled with bow, lyre and poetry as well as being a good friend to all. Handsome, but ruthless in battle, Apollo slew the mighty Cyclops. Other titles for this deity include god of divination and healing, god of song and lyre, god of pastures and flocks, god of fair wind for mariners, patron of physicians, as well as builder of cities. A beardless god, along with Ares, Hermes and Dionysus, Apollo was symbolized by the bow, quiver, shepherd's crook, swan and laurel. He purified people after they had committed criminal acts and overlooked, or concealed, obvious faults. Apollo was acclaimed to be the fullest measure of success.

Glyph: ♃⚷

Keywords for Apollo:

ascension	distances	infinity	opportunities
beams	expansive	knowledge	quantity
breadth	famous	mass production	scope
clone	glory	multiply	science
commerce	honors	music	space

ADMETOS

Admetos was a king of Pheras whose wife died in his stead. This king befriended Apollo during a time of need and was rewarded by being given immortality in exchange for affection. King Admetos was one of the argonauts following Jason in his quest. He won the hand of his goddess-wife by achieving the feat of driving a chariot drawn jointly by a lion and a wild boar hitched together, thus showing patience and control.

Glyph: ⚵

Keywords for Admetos:

adamant	darkroom	foundation	patience
bound	delay	grave	rock
closet	dense	granite	root
clot	durability	hollow organs	rotate
core	earthy	minerals	stable
crystals	ground	mining	stagnation
cycles	endurance	obstructions	suffocate

VULCANUS

Whether Vulcanus is related to the earlier Vulcan, to Greek Hephaestus or to Jewish Samson is the question. Vulcanus seems to mean the strength derived from cosmic forces which can be completely denied or withdrawn if certain rules are broken, as in the legend of Samson and Delilah. Vulcanus rocks foundations as it overpowers laws and governments.

Glyph: ♉

Keywords for Vulcanus:

anoint	dynamic	omnipotent	sustained
bellows	empowered	regimented	tornado
coercion	enormous	reserve	unleashes
compulsive	fated	superhuman	violence
controlled	mighty	supreme	volcanic

POSEIDON

Other names of this god of water and heaven include light carrier, the principle of divinity, god of earthquakes and god of the seas. Poseidon was carrier of the trident and became a bridge between heaven and earth. Unlike Neptune, this son of Kronos and Rhea is not considered to be muddled or emotional.

Glyph: ♓

Keywords for Poseidon:

abstract thought	floods	medium	revelation
bridge between the conscious and unconscious	genius	mental patient	sea
cognition	idea	novelty	spirit
creators	illumine	principle	television waves
divine spark	information	prophet	tidal waves
ethereal	inventor	propoganda	tranquil
	master	psychic	visualization

Chapter 3.

DELINEATIONS OF THE ASTEROIDS CERES, PALLAS ATHENA, JUNO AND VESTA

Delineations for midpoints and planetary pictures of the four major asteroids — Ceres, Pallas, Juno, Vesta — are given on the following pages. Although consistent data were found during the six years of research, there is certainly need and room for additional information concerning the asteroids in relationship to the traditional and transneptunian bodies used in astrology.

For astrologers not employing the technique of cosmobiology the following relationships may be considered as aspects.

There is not, to date, sufficient information to publish the midpoints between all the other planets and the asteroids. For example, results have been found in such cases as Sun/Moon equals Ceres but were not obtained for generational groupings such as the Uranus/Pluto equals Ceres. In time it is hoped that such information will become available.

The Ceres delineations are on pages 26 through 50.
The Pallas delineations are on pages 51 through 74.
The Juno delineations are on pages 75 through 97.
The Vesta delineations are on pages 98 through 119.

☿/M	Attitude toward domestic pets. Care of house plants. Occupied with seeding and growing. Ability to care for one's own body. Respect for dietary procedures. Innate reactions.

M — Same as above.

A — Believes in self-reliability. Communes with nature.

☉ — Healing abilities. Practical person. Personal hygiene. Medical doctor.

☽ — Nanny. Oriental Amah. Registered nurse.

☊ — Understands need for balance of schedule. Has an even amount of time for work and play. Surrounded by laborers.

♈ — Farmer. Blue collar worker. Belonging to the general middle class category. In the midst of your group or area. Mean.

☿ — Received a baby brother or sister. Sibling care.

♀ — Personal dietary habits. Health foods. Interest in nutrition.

♂ — Volatile disposition. Reacts impulsively. Expends much energy in physical labor.

⚷ — Same as above.

☿ — Practical about goals. Analyst. Common sense about personal hygiene. Self-disciplined at home and work.

⚶ — Desire for home and children. The nesting instinct is strong, and paternal urges dominate.

⚸ — Sees self as being persecuted. Unstable. Varies in mood from seeming to be a foolish prankster to a trusted employee.

♃ — Happy childbirth. Fortunate grandparents. Raised by foster parents. Good nurse or nursing care.

♄ — Involved in adoption procedures. Separated from the enlarged family.

⛢ — Employed as a nurse in a psychiatric unit.

♆ — Confused about self-worth and security. Self delusion. Lacking self-confidence and motivation.

♇ — Sees great changes and revisions in habits of civilization.

⚴ — Provincial artistic taste. Close family ties with cousins and grandparents. A 'Grandma Moses' potential.

⚵ — Able to create entities out of one's own subconscious.

⚶ — Dislike of war and military service. Conscientious objector.

♈ — Time of service on local jury. Mayor of small town.

♃Ⅱ — Completion of service oriented training.

⚻ — Feeling bogged down. Overloaded. Commitment completed in twice the anticipated time. Inner reserve used.

⚼ — Possessing strong will in time of stress.

⚳ — Faith which comes from parental training and example.

26

?/A	Nursing another person. Concern for others. Clinic, hospital or doctor's office. Greenhouse, nursery, window garden, garden plot, kitchen, nutritional laboratory, pet shop, drug or herb store, bakery or field. Adopted.

M — Role model for women. No-nonsense person. Understanding the plight of a friend. Sale of old house. Necessary contract.

A — Same as above.

⊙ — Male guardian. Influential friend concerned with a nutritional problem. Diet counselor. Rectal operation.

☽ — Maternal instincts worked out through caring for foster child.

☊ — Nursing or caring for old acquaintances through injury or grief.

♈ — Social worker. Adopted children made the headlines.

☿ — Raised by older brother or sister. Care of handicapped child not one's own. Raising a houseful of stepchildren.

♀ — Weight concerns related to hereditary glandular problem.

♂ — Energizes the whole unit of co-workers. Light touch covers sincere concern for others.

? — Same as above.

⚵ — Enjoys caring for others. Healer. Brings food to class. Reconstitutes. Hard-shelled business woman. Automatic acts.

⚸ — Hired to transport a small group of persons.

⚳ — Dedicated to charitable health care. Simple communion service. Sacrifice to nourish others. Relatives try to kidnap children.

♃ — Many close friends interested in healing techniques. Well-known physician.

♄ — Caring for older friends or parents. Born to elderly parents or giving birth past the middle of life.

♓ — Adopted child shocks and harms. Change in health patterns. Anxious about one's physical well-being.

♆ — Daydreams about welfare. Impractical diet. Confusing image of parent. Achieved a dream.

♇ — Helps others regenerate. Cultivates metaphysical activity. Intense reactions to changes in acquaintances.

⚴ — Synthetic gothic columns. Old fashioned charm. Friendly or gracious welcome.

⚷ — Finding old cookbooks at an auction. Restrictive diets.

⚵ — Fiery temper. Dress gunshot wound. Farm machinery. Combines or tractors.

⚶ — Paternal grandfather.

⚶ — Life in a harem. Living in a larger family compound. The extended family concept. Inauguration.

⚹ — Initiated into a select circle. Patience rewarded.

⚴ — Portrayed a very powerful image. Enforced dietary change.

⚺ — Baptismal godparents. Dreams of attracting a strong and loving protector.

? / ⊙	Objectivity toward the physical body. Not falsely modest, natural or untrained grace of body movement. Physical service. The daily regimen. Assimilation in upper intestines.

M — Nursed by a professional. Reaction from instinctive habits. Ideal nurturing.

A — Community centered attitude. Naive. Fresh, young looking face.

⊙ — Same as above.

☽ — Emotional confusion about one's ability to lead. Public stance. Rules as regent for sibling. Festive occasion, holiday dinner.

☊ — Gathering of like-minded people for banquet or refreshments.

♈ — Regal bearing yet not pompous. Leadership which expresses a homespun quality.

☿ — Quick perception, sometimes erroneous. Medical treatment of the scalp. = Neptune, reads Braille.

♀ — Child of a love match. Dominates with kindness. Male with many aunts. Loving parent. Relaxed, but reserved, body. Hospitable.

♂ — Overly concerned parent. Energy outlet inhibited. Cut seriously in accident. Appendectomy (= Jupiter/Mercury good outcome).

? — Same as above.

♀ — Woman suffrage leaders. Flow of authority. Abstract mathematics. Preparation of kneading bread. Health affected by job.

⚹ — Periods of being involved with home decorating.

↓ — Away from home much of the time. Irregular daily habits. Typical martyr complex. Body deprived of rest. Goal driven.

♃ — Having great faith. Heavy flow of blood. Excessive appetite. Growth of cysts, warts and benign tumors. Philanthropist.

♄ — Lack of grains or cereals. Bowel irregularity. Loss of father. Lack of a healthy male image.

♅ — Excitable, authoritarian. Sudden losses. Acts with a flourish. Eats at unusual times.

♆ — Healing by touch. Tends to starve the body at certain periods. Fasting. Ethereal appearance. = Mars, lacerated in accident.

♇ — Natural charisma. Creativity suppressed. Understands public.

⚴ — Birth of a long-awaited grandson. Lives near grandchildren.

⚵ — Menstrual or abdominal cramps. Feeling of self-contempt. Prefers to eat alone.

⚶ — Smoking habits. Unwilling to give up unhealthy habits for any reason. Selfish.

⚷ — Details handled by an attorney. Signed a complicated document.

⚷ — Culmination of diligence and hard work. Respected gardener. Receiving an earned title in ceremony. Day of ritual.

⚹ — Inner reserve. Removed from one's homeland by unforeseen circumstances.

⚸ — Typical ulcer personality. Bound by traditions and customs.

⚼ — Sees God in nature more than in organized religions.

♀/☽ (symbol)	Menial service such as a maid or laundress. Emotions about one's personal diet. Nursing others. Peaceful digestion, related to a cow chewing her cud. Adopted.

M — Healing by personal or spiritual faith. A gentle touch.

A — Around many single women or widows. Allied with the health food movements in some way.

☉ — Adopted by a substantial family. Supported publicly by friends and relatives. Welcomed with open arms.

☽ — Same as above.

☊ — Closely tied to maternal grandparents. Attached to the land.

♈ — Seen by the world as a concerned mother or parent. Tied to daily concerns. A home-centered existence.

☿ — Childlike faith and trust in relatives and neighbors.

♀ — Able to tune in to the responses of an audience. Sensitive to the reactions of others. Good timing sense.

♂ — Sometimes denies life. Surgical abortion. A vetoed farm bill. Cutting off support systems. Operating room nurse. Struggle.

♀ — Same as above.

♀ — Professional stepparent or foster parent.

⚸ — A nursing mother. A simple marriage ceremony. Proud parents.

☋ — Drainage of the head or sinus passages. Dedicated to group goal.

♃ — Treated by a competent medical team. Cheerfully obese.

♄ — Fame comes only through effort. Delay or denial of biological children. Lack of maternal love and support.

♅ — Accident prone. Concern for astrology. Working with women in the occult fields. Sudden breakup in the family. Weird guard.

♆ — Confusing or elusive girl child. Fluctuating moods.

♇ — Permanent change in household help schedule. Responds to the basic fears and needs.

⚴ — Member of a large family. Multiple births. Uninhibited affection for the family. Mother or sister a nurse.

⚵ — Serious digestive problems. Worries of a grievous nature.

⚸ — Draws cruel criticism to self from mother. Receives stings or smarts. Abused. Emotionally vulnerable.

⚶ — Foster parent. Block chairman. Roommother of PTA.

⚳ — Concerned with family counseling. Social worker.

⚷ — Fraudulent treatment of public trust. Impractical foundation.

△ — Surrounded by a friendly group in times of stress and emotional pressure. Extraordinary recuperative powers.

⚵ — An abiding faith in the face of disasters.

| ? / ♌ | Nurse's Guild. Parent Teacher's Association. Ecology groups. Nutritionist Council. Dietitians. Farmers' co-operatives. Nursery schools. Bonds of concern. |

M — Concerned with the destruction of land and air. Conserves.

A — Dairy associations. Baker or cook in the family.

☉ — Banding together for a common cause. These United States. Cooperative effort of physical entities. Land contract.

☽ — Teaches health through proper diet. Generous. Sympathetic. Cohesive influence on people in casts, clubs, or groups.

♌ — Same as above.

♈ — Receives awards or criticism for speaking out against issues.

☿ — Expressed concern for disadvantaged persons. Spokesman for a loosely organized group.

♀ — Fallopian tubes. Surrounded by beautiful and successful people.

♂ — Labor union membership and involvement.

? — Same as above

⚴ — Member of a home builder's association. Associated with the healing professionals. Investment in restored houses.

⚶ — Selling a home for sake of family harmony. Very sensitive to people's odors or attitudes.

⚼ — Takes own nutritional supplements to restaurants. Sold on benefits of health foods and vitamins. Megavitamins.

♃ — Concerned about world conditions. Civic minded.

♄ — Lives in seclusion. Nursed another through a serious, communicable disease. Segregated from the masses.

⚸ — Unexpected success explaining plight to large groups of people. Having a wry wit.

♅ — Deceived one's supporters. Actor in role of doctor or nurse.

♇ — Forms a simple association to transact business. A poorly devised group plan.

⚵ — A female associate justice. Composed in crowds. High moral character.

⚳ — Farm irrigation pipes. Connections cause worries. Destined to drive others away. Vicar of an old congregation.

⚷ — A collection of children's war games. Investigated an ancient racial conflict which still exists.

♇ — = Neptune, toppled from power by groups of commoners.

⚴ — Association for nurturing higher education and scientific research.

⚶ — Surrounded by belongings of the corpse.

⚸ — Forced to overcome one's natural shyness. Tendency to falter among strangers.

⚻ — Aligned with trained spiritual personnel. Eats with rabbi.

30

♇ /
♏ / ♈

National Health Organization. World grain exchange. General
nutrition. World Health Organization. Public health nurse.
A World's Fair. Ecology movements.

M — Under subtle influences. Memory of childhood events.

A — Member of an agrarian family. A certified medical professional. On the hospital staff. Health center worker.

☉ — Ruddy complexion. Possibly red hair. Rather insensitive skin.

☽ — Nationalized medical care. Concern for female acquaintances.
Interested in the tribal or public welfare.

☊ — Inherited characteristics.

♈ — Same as above.

☿ — Nun trained in medical care. Aroused by injustice seen. Speaks
out for healing methods. Holistic experiments. = Mars, race.

♀ — Time for leisure activities. Children in school. Responsibilities completed. Romance that attracts the press.

♂ — The Olympic games.

♐ — Same as above.

♀ — Mass inoculations to immunize against possible epidemic. Public
figure throughout life. Plague as part of public record.

⚹ — Recycles paper at public lectures. Denied physical motherhood.
Legally and publicly adopted children.

↓ — Dedicated to improving the public health. Award received for
nutritional discovery.

♃ — Parental with everyone. Good confessor. Sympathetic with
problems of comparative strangers.

♄ — Driven by the need to make a significant contribution to world.

♓ — Erratic habits caused by working with people of importance.

♅ — Isolated from normal activities by infirmities. Crippled yet
active. Able to sidestep issues.

♇ — Concealed ambition erodes health. Underlying tension in a
seemingly stable personality.

⚷ — Family business connections. Ordination ceremony. Bride of
the church. Wedding highly publicized. Pregnant bride.

⊕ — An impoverished nation in the news. National grain shortage.

⚸ — Setting up ambitious plans for the future.

⚶ — An important personage. Holds position of public authority.
Female government official.

⚳ — Graduate work in nutrition. Assistant to renown biochemist.

⚴ — Seasonal changes affecting the harvest. Undertakes a serious
commitment.

⚵ — Placed inadvertently near famous people. Speaker for the
National Cancer Foundation.

⚵ — Overly idealistic. Clean-cut public image. Enterprising
individual. Inner feelings exposed.

31

M — An elementary school teacher. Involved with nursery school.

A — Quick response. Clever sense of humor. Writes about daily
experiences. Shares personal journal.

☉ — Physical treatment around head area. Joyful disposition.
Gay but serious. Enjoys laughter.

☽ — Desires children. Elated about mailing manuscript. Receives
research paper from female. Teaches illiterate women.

☊ — Speaks against social injustices for women. Spokesman for
landed gentry. Farmer's representative. Founded Head Start.

♈ — Remembered in history for her ministry. Teacher and preacher.

☿ — Same as above.

♀ — Designed own home. Nervous tension causes metabolic unbalance
in digestion of sugars and starches. Women's liberation.

♂ — Working for future efforts.

? — Same as above.

♀ — Elementary school teacher. Rudiments of any subject. Direct
speaker or voice.

⚸ — Nervous headache. Raised a motherless child. Juvenile asthma.
Set up a park system. In favor of naturalist clubs.

☋ — Conversations deny personal wishes. = Mars, denies sex by
excessive chattering.

♃ — Dental assistant. Member of a surgical team. Child added
to the family.

♄ — Unable to show concern for others. Withdrawn. Hesitant in
speech or stride. Written farewell. Concerned about health.

♅ — Unexpected revisions of schedule. Clumsy hands.

♆ — Calm in the midst of confusion or squabble.

♇ — Transforms methods of communicating between homes. Teaches
in ancient symbols.

♃ — Fertile. Friendly and accomodating.

⚷ — Very selective. Speech affected by pressure in brain. Overly
critical. Worry self into an illness. Stricken nervous system.

⚵ — Development of a child.

⚶ — No-nonsense public representative. Deliberate speaker. Clever
spokesman.

⚴ — Capable extemporaneous speaker.

⚳ — Required to handle the daily grind. Thinks of the details
behind any event or movement.

⚕ — Writes and carries out orders from superiors. Keeps surgical
records in a hospital.

⚹ — Received acupuncture treatments. Sensitive nervous system
responds to medical systems. Good tactile sensations.

♃/♀	Balance of body and appetite needs. Naturally affectionate. Not self-indulgent. Soap-and-water complexion. Without additives. Impersonal love. Gentle touch.

M — Diet which tames the appetite.

A — Handsome physical appearance. Well-knit body and bones.

⊙ — Desiring to become self-supporting. Eating natural foods.

☽ — Beloved grandmother. Remembers early loss of physical mother. Parent of a girl child.

☊ — Raised by nurses and hospital staff. Early life spent in an institution. Away from biological parents. Joy to others.

♈ — Pictured as the example of a normal child. Catalog model.

☿ — Shows love and concern for neighbors and friends. Love letters. The woman's touch. Wife requested by letter rather than person.

♀ — Same as above.

♂ — Restores body balances. Physician and surgeon. Works in a homeopathic clinic. Healthy blood circulation.

♐ — Same as above.

⚵ — Intuitive about practical matters. Happy farmer. Love of horses. Healer. Veterinarian. Mathematical ability.

✠ — Too proper to express love. Autistic. Discreet use of cosmetics. Barriers to social intercourse. Burn scars.

⚻ — Innocent girl assaulted. Concern for the underprivileged takes much time and effort.

♃ — Gluttony. Born into a wealthy family. Inherited material assets.

♄ — Not hungry. Adviser to the lovelorn. Separated from his love by death.

♓ — Naturally affectionate at the wrong time. Forced to learn of health foods. Daily stress over daughter. Comedian.

♅ — Physical healing. Cosmetic surgeon. Health spas. Beauty resorts.

♆ — Developed a concern for ecology through landscape paintings. Wife ran the farm in his numerous absences. Revolutionary.

⚴ — The contented wife and mother. A happy and loving person.

⚷ — Torture of teenaged girl. Cruel death for a female. Misplaced trust of loved one.

⚸ — Sexually active and interested. Women accepted in the military services.

⚹ — Women in positions of authority.

⚶ — Sense of rhythm. Graceful body movements. Assisted a foreigner. Successful trade with homebuilders.

⚵ — The neglected body, especially of a woman.

⚳ — Deeply concerned with civil rights. Tremendous effort of a spastic to control bodily functions. High-powered salesperson.

⚻ — Worship of the Virgin Mary. Adoration of the saints.

♀/♂	Natural drive or flow of energy. Producing foods. Pep pills. Hard worker. Healing energies. Hospital surgery. Care of male child. Proper diet gives sustained energy.

M — Desperate. Aggravations noticeable. Directed toward self-destuction. Self depreciation. Appearance related to stress level.

A — Energy vampire. Female employer. Work schedule. A person who draws energy from those close around him or her.

⊙ — A surge of adrenaline. Hard work finally paid off. Crops growing abundantly. Loved to duel. A fighter.

☽ — Concern with muscle pain. Surgical nurse. Exercise improved physical well-being. Torn from maternal arms.

☊ — Works in a department store.

♈ — Good dancer. Founded national organization to advance health concerns.

☿ — Consulted a physician about muscle tension. Spirited supporter of school activities. Room mother.

♀ — Proud of fighters in titled family. Bear arms for personal beliefs. To work for the love of job.

♂ — Same as above.

♃ — Same as above.

☿ — Industrious employee. Sex after struggle. Rash sale of property.

⚵ — Beautiful home left unfinished because of circumstances. Document tied down with restrictions. Potential denied.

⚴ — Time of celibacy. Raised a grandchild. Unhibited energy. An incubator baby.

♃ — Generous grandfather or stepfather. Nourished by a machine. A respected family background.

♄ — Tension. Time of hard work. To nurse a shut-in. Skin eruptions. Overwork or excessive responsibilities. = M + Zeus, abused child.

♅ — Farm mishaps. Hospitalized for surgery following an accident. = Sun, care of male astrologer.

♆ — Received an anesthetic for an operation.

♇ — Forcing an issue of practical concern. Taking drastic action against parents or grandparents.

⚴ — To work in a family business. Tend to the details for many.

⚳ — Injured at work. Developed colitis from tension at work.

⚵ — Farm machinery. Mastectomy. Mechanically inclined.

⚶ — Women in factory positions. Lack of clear leadership.

⚴ — Musician. Practicing artist. Publicized her surgery.

⚵ — Delays farm work. Plowing the fields under for next season's planting.

⚴ — Extremely fortunate. Breaks through strong barriers. Overcomes prejudices. Elected despite overwhelming odds.

⚹ — Practical approach to religion.

♃ / ♀	Farmer. Ecologist. Practical nurse. Exploring nature's depths. Meticulous. Veterinarian. Home economist. Florist. Body mechanism or immunity. Leaned on a tree. Coordinated.

M — Time of being anointed. Authority handed over from above.

A — Friendly. Easy going appearance. Clean outlook on life.

☉ — At ease heading one's profession. Born leader. Flow of authority. Day of honor. Day in the limelight. Supreme court.

☽ — Associates emotionally involved. Trusting. Naive. Sucked a thumb late in life. Stuffing a goose to make pate.

☊ — Shared working methods. Visited and studied other projects of like nature. Sent workers around the world.

♈ — Farm news reported.

☿ — Makes his or her living as a mood actor or actress.

♀ — Career woman. Pleasant. High resistance to communicable diseases. To own one's own business.

♂ — Enjoys hard work and a sense of accomplishment.

♁ — Same as above.

♀ — Same as above.

⚥ — Married to one who is involved in nurturing others. Worker feels thwarted. Resents sexual suppression. Cosmetic sales.

☿ — Sacrifices many hours of pleasure for career. A truly dedicated worker.

♃ — Prosperous farmer. Physical or mental builder. Fortunate patron of the arts.

♄ — Lack of immunity. Classroom suppresses creativity. Can't have plants in one's office because of allergies. Viral disease.

♅ — Inventor. Household appliances run by motor or electricity.

♆ — Founded hospitals and orphanages where there were none. Protected established church leaders during religious controversy.

♀ — Works in public service. Mass consciousness. Liaison between farm community and government.

♇ — A supportive network. Sons and daughters rallied to parents' side during illness.

⊕ — Crusader against social injustice. A spokesman for the underprivileged.

⚡ — Shocking disclosure. Spearhead for reform movement. Parched earth. Promoted the increase of parks.

♈ — Owner of potentially desirable real estate. Wealthy child.

♃Ⅱ — Practical experience as training rather than college degree.

⚕ — Interpreted the theological concept of affection. Sturdy.

♌ — Self confident. Ability to adapt to strange surroundings.

♓ — Grateful for small blessings. A peaceful working day. Time of Thanksgiving for a good harvest.

♃/♍	Instinctive self discipline. Nutritious dinners. Simple entertaining. Harvest fairs and celebrations. Amish style dress. Childbirth. Provincial customs.

M — Works primarily with conservative housewives.

A — Surrounded by the family at a wedding or engagement party.

☉ — Categorizing and simplifying one's life style. Elimination of useless debris. Believes quality rather than quantity.

☽ — The mother's health changed family habits and diet. The wives arrived.

☊ — Handles organic cleaning formulas. Sells supplements to wives. Concerned with general well-being of the public.

♈ — Tells interesting dinner stories without ever being "off color."

☿ — Yells at mate out of own frustration. Elegant sense of humor. Not patient with stupid people. Does not suffer fools gladly.

♀ — Quarrels with females. A bossy sister. Dominated by mate.

♂ — Crusades for social legislation.

? — Same as above.

⚨ — Group compaigning for equal rights. Formal organization or association. Joyous occasion.

⚶ — Same as above.

☋ — Thwarted by family responsibilities. Ambitions criticized. Censured by peers.

♃ — Fortunate legal aspects of contract. Awarded a spectacular career opportunity. Signed document gladly.

♄ — Divorced. Practical and harsh in relationships. Long term illness. Lack of fertility.

♅ — Hard to establish contact. Child of strict parents. Pancreas infected. Complications during pregnancy.

♆ — Abnormal growth spurts because of glandular disfunction.

♇ — Born into wrong generation to fulfill leadership potential.

♃ — Personal life has definite bearing on physical health.

⚷ — Serious demeanor. Part of impressive, ancient ceremony.

⚳ — Good team worker. Group involved in fighting a fire. Explosion potential.

⚀ — Vows. Accepting a formal commitment. Requesting legal advice about documents involved. Inauguration as ustice.

⚴ — Mental snob.

⚵ — Attachment to home leads to misery later in life. Family is all important.

△ — Quick mind. Sharp tongue. Capable of disciplining self in the face of personal disappointment.

⚸ — Self reliant. Sees the Divine in others.

♃ ↙ ↓	Resignation. Loss of home and family. Sacrifice of life. Denial of the fullness of living. An understanding of nature's bounty and famines.

M — Gives up much to achieve long-range plans. Not changed by success.

A — Aunt raised child while mother worked. Hospital stay for recovery. Inhibited emotions. Discouraged family. Lack of love.

☉ — Serious young person. Solemn but sympahhetic. A nun or deacon.

☽ — Appeared as grasping opportunist. Away from society and friends because of family demands.

☊ — Prefers to be concerned with the underprivileged of the world.

♈ — Desire for material power led to separation from higher spiritual values. Cannot be known as a positive person.

♀ — Barren or denied biological children.

♀ — Periods of celibacy. Lack of affection. Health spa or resort. Eventual defeat.

♂ — Abortion. Miscarriage. Denial of life. Publicly consecrated to holy service.

? — Same as above.

☿ — Willing to serve. Survives despite susceptibility to diseases. A sickly childhood.

⚥ — A marriage where there is very little love and affection.

↓ — Same as above.

♃ — A life of much suffering and denial. Many deaths. Empathetic.

♄ — Forced to resign. Motivation misunderstood. All achievements through hard struggles.

♅ — Gave up luxurious home to pursue personal beliefs. Children reared by grandparents. Focused on unusual concepts.

♆ — Onset of puberty delayed by serious illness. Fragmented. Deceit and fraud of simple people.

♇ — Concerned with physical deformities and health changes.

⚳ — Away from the enlarged family because of business demands.

⚷ — Forced to become involved in archeological dig.

⚴ — Death by fire. Plane imploded upon ground contact. Burned.

⚶ — Fraud by leaders. Mismanagement.

⚵ — Birth of a child in a foreign country. Different cultures.

⚸ — Very hard working. Bearing children under primitive conditions. Infant mortality rate. Meticulous and deliberate.

⚹ — Forced into periods of solitude.

⚺ — Uses the higher powers in the wrong way at times. Blown fuses. Bankrupt institution.

37

<table>
<tr><td>♄/♃</td><td>Homespun philosopher. Bountiful harvest. Many useful gifts. Practical generosity. Kindly stepfather. Fortunate adoption. Entrance into good family.</td></tr>
</table>

M —	Tends to starve self when worried or under stress
A —	Community support and endeavors. Uncomplicated plans. Full backing of associates and relatives.
☉ —	A nation rejoiced at his birth. Birth of an heir. Talented.
☽ —	Ability to present natural concepts publicly. Assisted mother in caring for orphans.
☊ —	Rising to the heights through the ffforts of associates. At the disposal of superiors. Connected with grass-roots movements.
♈ —	Devoted parent. Ambitious. Prolific gardener renown for prize-winning fruits. Known for charitable works with women.
☿ —	Meticulous childhood records kept. Prolific writer. Primary developmental steps for an author. Elementary maturation process.
♀ —	Green thumb with houseplants. Cheerful homemaker.
♂ —	Heals with flower remedies. Herbalist. Taken into a military family. Birth of sons or grandsons.
⚴ —	Same as above.
⚶ —	Body immune system overtaxed. Reaction to immunization.
⚵ —	Bridal shower. Fortunate and fruitful marriage. Business and holiday combined, with mate. Married to fellow religious worker.
⚳ —	Birth pangs. Problems with blood sugar regulation.
♃ —	Same as above.
♄ —	Harvest only after hard work or much effort expended. Death of foster father.
♅ —	Practical use of astrology and occult sciences. Sudden and romantic wedding. Pilot crashing plane.
♆ —	Uncertain about size of crop or deceived concerning results. Woman minister. Father with an alcohol problem.
♇ —	Agitation within "Mother Church." Heart of religious issue.
⚷ —	Lighthearted picnic or simple social occasion.
⊕ —	Luck with raw materials.
⚸ —	Remodeling delayed because of legal restrictions. Accepting the practical solution. Acquires promotions early in life.
⚳ —	Received a passport or visa. Travels on the job.
⚴ —	Fortunate to have such a wide choice of good baby sitters. Day of supreme court inauguration.
⚥ —	Calm in face of difficult world conditions.
△ —	Trauma resulted in positive approach to life. Success achieved through tremendous effort. Faith or spiritual healing.
✕ —	Simple religious faith which "moves mountains."

♃/♄	Grain shortage. Extremely responsible. Aged grandparents. Loss of weight. Took grandchild to raise. Chilled to the bone. Molested by older man. Fear of uncontrolled fertility.

M — Feels responsible for harm or injuries to self and others.

A — Concern for family burdens. Complaints from relatives.

☉ — Well preserved in old age. Detached air. Raised strictly. Rationing of resources.

☽ — Pain of swollen knees relieved by medical dietary modifications. An old woman.

☊ — Delay. Poor judgment in public affairs. Associated with older people. Concerned with stepchildren.

♈ — Losses become public knowledge. Responsibility for urging people to boring, but needed action.

☿ — Autistic. Hesitancy to speak. Lack of natural communication.

♀ — Separated from sister or female relatives. Loss of maternal grandmother. Recovered from acute chilling.

♂ — Responsible application of energy. Killing the illusion. Exposed to physical interference and restraint.

♃ — Same as above.

♀ — Bravery in the face of danger. Responsibility for future life. Established recovery procedures. Service oriented.

⚴ — Pancreas infection cured only by diet.

↓ — Periods of chastity.

♃ — Blow to the body. Liver involved in illness.

♄ — Same as above.

♓ — Reformer. Inspired by devout family upbringing.

♅ — Use of synthetic sweetner.

♇ — Pilot misjudged distance from the ground. Altitude problems. Balance affected.

⚵ — Division or problems within the family unit.

⊕ — Ordained for service. Separated from family closeness. Serious commitment. Helping underprivileged. Facing obstacles.

⚶ — Loss of garden or farm produce, by fire or insect invasion.

♈ — Feminine interests on leadership team. Overpowered by nature. Death or injury by act of God.

♃Ⅱ — Biochemical abnormalities cause severe allergies.

⚷ — Illness or death of a grandparent. Ancestral land.

⚸ — Airplane rammed into a treetop. Dietary restrictions.

♓ — Dire need for self-control. Tendency toward depression.

39

Won't humor people or compromise. Inconsistent parent.
Hide or tone down shocking ideas. Mother or care for people.
Unusual diet or food intake. Practical ingenuity.

M — Deliberate and calm even in emergencies. Inauguration of justice.

A — Small group to nurture new ideas. Useful application of astrological principles.

☉ — Non-compromising. Not antagonistic to ideals of others. Reclaims losses. A seeking heart. Enterprising.

☽ — Withdrawn from family circle. Lack of parental attachment. Controlled emotions. Strong willpower.

☊ — A shock to the body system.

♈ — Provincial. Unique public health care facility.

☿ — Journal of family practice. The young medical technician or X-ray operator. News of nutritional discovery.

♀ — Daily stress over daughter or sister. Metabolic problems resulting from worry or overwork. Blood sugar fluctuations.

♂ — Abrupt change in hormone level. Cautious about dietary habits.

? — Same as above.

⚲ — Polite request for freedom. Independent actions against an authority figure. Shock to immune system.

⚼ — Inconsistencies in the marriage. Nervous stomach. Spastic.

⚷ — Stood staunchly for beliefs. Defeated attempt at election by being adamant about personal ideals.

♃ — Using unorthodox methods to aid the needy. Not sympathetic to philanthropic display. Minister in an unusual position.

♄ — Has tendency to escape when not in control of situation. Reaction to strange foods. Allergies set off.

♅ — Same as above.

♆ — Mediumship used for mundane affairs. Sleeps or reads as an escape mechanism when disappointed. Self hypnosis.

♇ — Purged through a desire to conform.

♃♀ — Creative. Sensitive to art, music and beauty. Desires to live in harmony.

⊕ — Sudden destruction of body tissue. Forceful eruption.

⚸ — To treat people roughly. Brusque manner.

♈ — Being managed from behind the scenes. Childhood training affects adult decisions and leadership capacities.

♃♊ — Paradoxical. Pseudo-alliances. Highly unstable. Natural tendency to expand uproars. Falsely appears to cooperate.

⚵ — Cyclic deviations. Crop failures due to climatic changes.

△ — Exposed to some potent esoteric practices. Remains calm in face of dramatic events. Impeccable sense of timing.

⚹ — Comfortable on TV. Unpredictable search for truth. Unexpected spirituality. "Born-again" Christian. Daily prayer.

40

| ♃/♆ | Practical idealist. Confusion about health matters. Alcoholic relatives. Improper diet causes allergies. Druid. Strongly intuitive. Healing and nursing interests. |

M — Looking at daily duties in a practical, yet optimistic way. Subconsciously affected by mother or childhood nurse.

A — News or gossip about medical problems. Hypochondria.

☉ — False sense of security. To relax the body completely. Fall down harmlessly. Different from the majority of persons.

☽ — Period of depression. Emotions which affect the health. A dream state existing during conscious periods.

☊ — Isolated from people. Withdrawal because of unfounded fears.

♈ — Diseases spread through water or air. General uncleanliness of an area or a group of people.

☿ — Speaks in riddles. Explains activity by symbolism. Brings understanding out of confusion.

♀ — Temperance. Food can be a substitute for companionship and affection. Disappointments released through eating.

♂ — Fraudulent. Fought against predicted farm breakdown. Untrue procedures.

♁ — Same as above.

⚥ — Seeks counseling about methods of parenting. Protective about religious or philosophical comrades.

⚛ — Disappointed in marriage. Wed to immature film star. Emotional inbalance in a relationship.

⚴ — To reach the end of one's patience. Metabolic disturbance. Dedicated marine biologist.

♃ — Gained an alcoholic stepparent or guardian

♄ — Uncertain about purpose or goal. Restrictions. Health problems. Preventing freedom of action.

♅ — Fortunate in the face of famine. Supportive of transoceanic flights. Entertains by impersonating dignitaries.

♆ — Same as above.

♇ — The plague. Dissolving family ties in a final way. Idealistic concepts create upheaval.

⚵ — Combines the use of medicine with common sense for cures.

⚶ — Morbid cares. Left to clean up from past confusion. Followed parental inefficiency with psychological treatment.

⚷ — Hiking. Back packing in the wilderness. Blew-up at criticism.

⚳ — Founder of unorthodox religious group. A woman minister in times of male domination.

⚴ⅠⅠ — Formal training in biochemistry. Negation of a college degree.

⚸ — Poison or chemicals added to foodstuffs.

⚘ — Driven by higher motives. Diligent goals not easily perceived. Receives inner satisfaction.

⚹ — Out of body experiences. Floating-on-air sensation. Operating anesthetia. Extended periods of emotional withdrawal.

♇/♀	Overconcern with details hinders cooperation. Aging mother. Changing schedule. Care of the elderly or infirm. A woman rebel in time of male supremacy.

M — Considering oneself to be victimized. Problems in the face of authority.

A — Looks to the biological family for support and protection. Functional disorders.

☉ — Transformation of daily life plan. Impersonating a doctor. Creating a medical character.

☽ — Resentment of nagging mother. Digestive processes hindered by disruptions. Faced away from mother figure.

☊ — Bankrupt. Fluctuating commodities. Upset the world monetary balance. Isolationist politics.

♈ — Scandal. Disruptive to many persons. Reporting of the destruction or bombing of health facilities.

☿ — Much discussion leads to drastic measures. New medication attempted in desperation.

♀ — Birth pangs. Anxiety of burdens accepted.

♂ — Resumed medication for hormone inbalance. Naturally impulsive. Florid coloring of skin.

♂ — Same as above.

☿ — New career opportunities. Public opinion denied favored plans.

⚷ — Chauvinistic attitude from mate supresses natural talents. Cares for in-laws. Meticulous. Disturbs spouse. Frigid.

☋ — Permits severe domination of character by others.

♃ — Success came out of another's death. Blood disorders. Fed and taught the poor and impoverished. Respected women.

♄ — Natural food kick. Desire for grains and cereals.

♓ — Creates turmoil. Erratic spadework for a project.

♆ — Cauterized seeping wounds. Criticized papal power. Purge. Prays in seclusion. Calls for reform of established church.

♆ — Same as above.

⚴ — Upheaval for many families. Homes suddenly broken up. Family members lost in catastrophe.

⊕ — Ministering to disturbed persons. Counseling troubled ones.

⚸ — Seeing very little purpose to life. Concern with the reproductive system.

♈ — Lack of authority. Frustrated by leadership inadequacies.

⚵ — A survey of revolutions.

⚳ — Takes moves calmly in stride. Release of emotional frustration through creative husbandry, gardening. Blocked traits.

⚶ — Working through a powerful force. Prayer of anguish.

♓ — Impoverished childhood leads to escapism through dreams or religious extremes.

♀/♃⚥	Naturally affectionate and loving. Harmonious marriage. Farm cooperative. Family oriented. Pleasant. Fun loving. Foster parents or family.

M — Involved in family duties or responsibilities. Beloved one.

A — Related to a family living on the land in a simple way. Life in a tent. Nomadic.

☉ — Nursed by relatives. Home remedies. Healing herbs. Affection between male relatives. Close ties. Brotherly love. Summer.

☽ — Practical wife or mother. Nurses in the family. Gentle. Public acknowledgment of female role.

☊ — Connected with a simple family life.

♈ — Family business. Renown farmer. Strongly affected by immediate family conditions. Born to famous, unspoiled parents.

☿ — Familar habits. Created schools of common thought. Literary family. Group with similar concepts of everyday living.

♀ — Females in charge of merger. Inherited from the maternal side of the family.

♂ — Meeting of all involved parties to work out details. Children married to different nationalities and moved far away.

♃ — Same as above.

⚲ — Accepting vestments of religious community. First lady priest. Achieving rights for self and others.

⚷ — The happy wedding ceremony. Wed to one's beloved. Intimate.

☋ — Gratitude denied. Uncooperative out of personal hurt. Withdrawn. Early parental separation. Denied unified responses.

♃ — Associates comfortably with the married state.

♄ — Family grief over child's death. Congenital defect. Chronic hereditary illness. Turns to family in tragedy and sorrow.

♆ — Changes in family behavior. Sudden and unexpected breakup of the family unit.

♆ — Concern for parental misfortune. Mourns for return of old traditions. Remembers the past.

♇ — Compassion for family's upheaval. Shared grief.

♇ — Same as above.

⊕ — Disappointment concerning plans for a lovely home. The sad relatives. Separations for natural causes.

⚳ — Fertile husband or wife. Time of conception. Preparations.

♈ — Legal unifications. Pronouncements by persons in positions of authority. Pleasant employer.

♊ — Married a classmate or business partner. Joined a prominent group or association. Fraternal.

⚥ — Delays giving affection in marriage. Dead relationship. Community shocked by deaths. Accidental separation, but timely.

♎ — Powerful emotional need for parental harmony.

♓ — Dreams of finding soul mate. Impractical about responsibilities. Sees beauty in spite of hardships.

43

| ? / ⊕ | Sensible about death. Diseased colon. Shell of a house. Death or depression of grandparent. Infested home. Filthy living conditions. Bedbugs. House needing repairs. |

M — Feeling of disgust with one's personal appearance. Dislike of daily habits.

A — Takes on problems of another. Erases errors. Hears confessions. Absolves or condemns.

☉ — Successful criminal lawyer. Helped start a home for orphan mountain girls.

☽ — Reacted out of fear. Diseased colon. = Cupido, death of maternal grandmother or grandfather.

☊ — Associating with accused criminals. Murderous contacts. Domestic court cases.

♈ — Sympathy for unknown victims.

☿ — Speaks about need for purification of the body and daily regimen. Shy about appearing publicly. Lonely and gentle.

♀ — Love in the confines of a harem or group. Lack of spontaneous warmth.

♂ — Removal of colon, surgical procedure. Digestion ails. Escape from impoverished background. Primitive environment.

? — Same as above.

♀ — Parted from peers and family by career obligations.

⚧ — Concerns caused by problems or ill health of the spouse.

↓ — Denial of biological parenthood. Loss of antiques. An old or historical home.

♃ — Ruptured colon. Merry or "grass" widow. Nutritional problems associated with overeating.

♄ — Close of an era in history. Remains needing eradication.

♅ — Legal shambles. Self indulgent. Overcoming formidable obstacles by patient efforts.

♆ — Close of the silent film era. Overwrought by emotions.

♇ — Legal advisor for estates and divorce cases.

⚴ — Born into an impoverished environment. Abused child. One of a slum family.

⊕ — Same as above.

⚸ — Ruptured colon. Drain infected surface forcibly. Puncture of intestinal wall. Invades diseased area and tissues.

♈ — City authorities restricted building plans. Sale of an old house which needs many repairs.

♃II — Welfare programs administered locally.

⚶ — Abusive and deliberate weight gain for revenge. Required to live on strict diet for serious medical problems.

⚷ — Festering or polluted beyond repair or cleansing. Abrasive.

♓ — Deepest concern for diseased persons. Finding perspective in mythology. Psychological undercurrents.

44

⚷ / ⚷	Useful energies. Fires which are tamed to be used. Farm machinery. Well-trained under strict discipline. Social activist.

M — One who respects the military principles and methods.

A — Born into a position of leadership. From royal parentage. Of the ruling class. Peerage.

☉ — Leaders of the trainees. Extremely aggressive. Untrained Master. = Vesta, died in airplane explosion.

☽ — Emotional responses brought under control.

☊ — Associated with disciplined activities. Strict regimen of life. Primarily adult endeavors.

♈ — Congenial leaders or foremen. Accepts responsibility calmly, especially in times of trauma.

☿ — Excellent creative actress. Capable of mastering many roles during a lifetime.

♀ — Blessed and cherished by many grandchildren.

♂ — The enlisted or military man. Working with machinery on the assembly line. Household electrical equipment.

⚵ — Same as above.

⚢ — Candlemaking. Gets into the matter quickly. Manages an efficient office. Allows for few interruptions to work.

⚸ — Born to a farm family. People who appreciate and respect nature. Close-knit relationship. Ties forcefully closed.

⚴ — Ability to deny desires to accomplish goals.

♃ — Imaginative. Charismatic. Makes the ridiculous seem possible.

♄ — Works long hours. Perseveres. Likes to be on top of every situation. Conservative spokeswoman.

♅ — Jealous of good fortune of another. Experiments with planting methods. Involves others in preventive methods. Defensive.

♆ — Expressed jealousy for other members of a group. Discontented with personal achievements.

♇ — Controversial promoter of social changes. Rapid revisions of duties. Focused attention on necessary reforms.

⚵ — Created lovely quilts out of dress scraps. Proud donor of beautiful handiwork.

⊕ — Overcooked or burned by intensity of drive. Charred.

⚸ — Same as above.

♈ — Forceful leader. Unsophisticated yet charismatic legislator. Speaker for own group. Promoted farm bills.

♃♊ — Educated in a military elementary or high school. Military professor.

⊕ — Mismanagement undermined the structure.

⚼ — Miracles, whether deadly or healing. Powerful and explosive people and situations.

♓ — Strict adherence to the religious beliefs of the family.

45

♄/♈	Pastoral care or counseling. Dietary interest or authority. Untrained healer. Entered nurse's training. Compassionate counselor.

M — Simple understanding of the laws of nature. Gracious acceptance of the inevitable. Calm.

A — Responsible for the care of all of his or her immediate family members. Cares for those in the vicinity.

☉ — Authorities must be involved in the planning stages. Piloting a ship as well as a project. Base of spine chakra.

☽ — Concerned leadership. Ordained by the bishop. Cared for by women. Women in positions of command.

☊ — Grandfather respected by acquaintances. Born into a simple, but honorable family.

♈ — Destined to lead or command at some time of life.

☿ — Tonsils removed surgically. Hesitancy in speech. Chronic tension in the throat area.

♀ — Organized a program of color therapy and demonstrated its practical usage. Clear, strong singing voice.

♂ — Hard worker. Having a "green thumb" with plants. Oversees the storage of foodstuffs.

♂ — Same as above.

♀ — Manager of a farm or dairy. Food processor

✠ — Wed to provincial people. Dominated by spouse. A time of learning humility

↓ — Passes up promotions and acclaims. Well coordinated.

♃ — Jury duty. Involved in lawsuits or small claims court.

♄ — The aging process. Forced to live on a restricted diet. Defective metabolic regulation in the body.

♅ — Sudden upsets in farm products or prices.

♆ — Confusion with the grain market. Dealing primarily with the oats crops. Liquor licenses.

♇ — Authority on diets and weight control. Toppled from a high office by changes in government leadership.

♃♀ — Family or divorce counselor. Treated by a relative.

⊕ — Dissolving or prohibiting by government order. Divorce or separation. Policy breakdown.

⚵ — Good manager of meager resources.

♈ — Same as above.

♃⚼ — Spokesman for educational fund drive. Backs favored legislation. Teacher elected to high office. Apprenticed.

⚵ — Breakdown of local government structure. Unwise taxes.

⚳ — Deals comfortably with persons in positions of authority. Copes with emergencies well. Head of enlarged family.

⚴ — Full of vim and vigor. Bountiful energies. Natural psychic or spiritual healing abilities.

♀ / ♃⚷	The Great Plains. Biochemistry. Market Place. Acres of grain fields. Advanced dietary study. Compassionate. Chief of staff in hospital ward.

M — To enter business affiliation with faith and respect. Nurse.

A — Associated with scholars. Shy. Expect others to be trustworthy.

☉ — Surrounded by spiritualists. Acvanced medical techniques used. Sustaining of life.

☽ — Academic public duties. Early life on a farm. Women's offspring.

☊ — Connected with a hospital. Owned by a close-knit group. Co-operative ownership.

♈ — Involved with investments or banking. Public knowledge.

☿ — Serious study through personal investigation. Nature study.

♀ — Adored by female relatives and friends. One of a pair of twin girls. Cheerful. Benevolent.

♂ — Works as a registered nurse in large hospital. Medical person.

♃ — Same as above.

⚷ — Play periods observed by psychiatrists and sociologists. Enjoyed keeping a journal. Daily diary of childhood activities.

⚸ — Precise technician. Good record keeper.

☋ — Education delayed due to family problems. Reading difficulty.

♃ — Renown healer. Used a profusion of restoration techniques. A scholar of ancient wisdom.

♄ — Illness because common-sense care of the body was ignored.

♅ — X-ray training. Played the clarinet. Unexpected methods used in saving a life.

♆ — Chairman of counseling team. Puts daydreams into practice.

♇ — Knowledge of purging by natural methods. Study of nutrition and human behavior.

⚷ — Art therapy course. Comes from farm family background. Rural environment. Amish.

⊕ — Study and evaluation of depression periods.

⚵ — Innovative professional. Deals with challenges calmly. Not ashamed to call in trained help or aides.

♈ — The study of business management. On-the-job training.

♃⚷ — Same as above.

⚶ — Not using advanced training to greatest advantage. Schooling delayed. Physical condition limits food intake.

⚶ — Efforts of the mother rewarded.

⚻ — Changes necessary during spiritual development period. A time of fasting.

47

♃/♇	Seasons of the year, month or life. Planting by the cycles. Planned parenthood. Winter. Good timing. Sensitive to the clock or calendar. Well grounded. Common sense.

M — Guided by concepts of concealed timing. Understanding limits.

A — Pleasing architecture. Surrounded by stable, older people. To know authority as an outward constituent of self-discipline.

☉ — Delegated to menial tasks. Forced to wait for recognition of achievements. Grandfather of retarded grandchild.

☽ — Empathetic to changing moods. Flows with the times and circumstances. Not outwardly emotional.

☊ — Associated with persons of common sense and good judgment.

♈ — Receives recognition for working with abused or retarded children. Known as a sensible person.

☿ — Periodic depressions. Active in psychic phenomena. Stirs up co-workers, sometimes in an underhanded manner.

♀ — Cosmetic changes recommended. Hair shaved off for medical purposes. Plain but pleasant.

♂ — Decorates for the holidays. Works according to the weather. Seasonal employment. Menial tasks.

♁ — Same as above.

☿ — Funeral director or counselor. Conveniently absent when trouble strikes. Negotiator. = Mercury, basically insecure.

⚴ — Long-term illness diagnosed. Cost of discipleship.

⚳ — Retains objectivity despite personal relations. Exclusive assignments. Minutely documented growth of rare patients.

♃ — Peace of mind. Modest future. Farm boy elected to high office. Backed by building contractors. Man of simple origins.

♄ — Dangers are overcome by holding to one's inherent beliefs.

♅ — Unique approach to diagnosing congenital defects. Concerned with physical abnormalities. Aroused suspicion.

♆ — Trapped in a heavy fog. Mist caused pilot to lose sense of direction. Danger of serious injury.

♇ — Emerging to the brink of an abyss. Upheavals of the earth.

⚴ — Product of a broken or unhappy home. Abused child or abusing parent or caretaker.

⚷ — Periodic caring for disabled children and adults. Miscarriage. Unfortunate termination of pregnancy.

⚸ — Occasional cleansing of the body impurities by such methods as fasting or purging.

♈ — Testified at murder trial. Pressure on one's superior. Prominent figure placed in difficult situation.

⚵ — Small, crowded agricultural college. Limited education.

⚶ — Same as above.

⚴ — Lost control. Fog disguised familiar landmarks. Destruction by another. Tragic circumstances.

♓ — Helped others in spiritual development. Surrounded by spirit children or teachers.

<table>
<tr><td>♁/⚸</td><td>Compelled to reevaluate daily regimen. In control of the body functions. Strict habits and training. Subordinate to the hospital staff. Medical chief of staff.</td></tr>
</table>

M — An authoritative mother or nursemaid.

A — Associated closely with important personages. Sells metaphysical supplies. Lenient.

☉ — Focus of attention. Induced abortion.

☽ — Required to be inactive or in the bodily care of another. Saturn, placed in nursery school because of mother's ill health.

☊ — Belonging to diet group. Subordinate to little understood associate. Rare blood type.

♈ — Medical news bulletin acclaiming unusual treatment and success.

☿ — Speaking with a tight, clipped manner.

♀ — Under government custody. Beyond human care and control.

♂ — Military intervention. Working under pleasant, but disciplined conditions. Medical technicians.

? — Same as above.

⚥ — Welfare movements. Adroit politician. Progressive leadership. Powerful figure or administrator.

⚴ — Restricted movements. Childhood paralysis abated by puberty.

☋ — Forced to disband. Closed by intervention of authorities. An unaccepted religion or association.

♃ — Miraculous recoveries from serious physical injuries. Multiple interests.

♄ — Loss of control. The need to show humility around peers.

♅ — Unexpected aid from the administration. Compelled to consort with the defendant.

♆ — Tried to excape from constant public scrutiny. Unable to control one's own emotions without drugs.

♇ — Subconscious resentments affect health adversely. Life style changed abruptly by whim of others.

♃ — Tremendous need for family security and solidarity.

♷ — Spiritual healer unearthed old methods. Tricked by realtor. Antiquarian. Discovered in temple ruins.

⚵ — Superior nursing care. Help from determined persons. Focus on universal concepts directs attention.

♇ — Propelled from humble origin to association with world leaders. Humble in presence of pomp and glory.

♃Ⅱ — Life story enjoyed and followed by multitudes of people. Easy acclaim for achievements.

♇ — Limitations placed upon one of advanced years. Restrictions.

△ — Same as above.

♓ — Cares for the underpriviledged. Actively compassionate. Perceptive. Spiritual awareness. Occult student.

M — Instinctive reactions in times of trauma. Interest in female mythology or religious cults.

A — Simple religions, using very little ritual and music.

☉ — Euphoric state. Ingestion of drugs. Trance. Dealing with deceit. Injects pain-killers. Day of confusion. Vulnerable.

☽ — Genuine concern about raising the common man's standards. Empathy with people's physical and spiritual needs.

☊ — A mediator.

♈ — Unrealistic about demands necessary to achieve even a minor victory. Unreasonably accomodating.

☿ — Signing papers in good faith. Seeks spiritual peace. Ultrasonic sound waves.

♀ — Selling house on a hunch. Taking advice of older woman on faith. Intuitive directions.

♂ — Idealistic struggle.

♃ — Same as above.

♀ — Espousing a charitable cause or endeavor.

⚸ — Shared periods of worship or meditation between spouses.

☋ — Daily experiences among strangers. = Hades, psychic esperiences affirmed during a murder trial.

♃ — Volunteer work within the church. Care of the altar.

♄ — Separation from utopian environment. Loss of personal time. Pilot failed mission. Lack of spiritual pursuits.

♅ — Revelation in religious practices. Sudden comprehension

♆ — Looking at the greater potential without estimating the cost. Etheric field warped. Misjudge details on extensive project.

♇ — Dietary change for spiritual advancement.

♃ — Member of a religious association. On retreat with family members or close friends. Healing with colors.

⊕ — Delve deeply into the distant past through intuition. Too idealistic in practical affairs.

⚷ — Incorporate music and rhythm into healing sessions. Concerned about health and diet.

♈ — An authority on spiritual training and discipline. Teacher of mediums or clairvoyants.

♃Ⅱ — Pilot of aircraft. Professional aviator. Share dreams of ideal society. Visionary leader. Culture shock sensitivity.

♀ — Highly organized professional. Modulated life. Person who can handle national matters competently. Well honed,brillant.

⚶ — Superior understanding. Guardian angel. Godparents.

⚹ — Same as above.

50

☿ / M	Professional goals. Personal ambition and desires. Dexterity. Attitude twoard recycling ideas and equipment. Common sense. Inventiveness. Objectivity. Career honors.

M — Same as above.

A — Pleasant appearance. Dresses appropriately. Professional.

☉ — Self-confident. Talented. Natural charm and grace. Inner defenses and disciplines. Jr. High School science teacher.

☽ — Housekeeper. Career oriented woman. Realtor. Foster parent. Verbalized objectives.

☊ — Connections with leading businessmen. Career assistance from associates.

♈ — Honors received for accomplishments.

☿ — Newspapers to be recycled. Accepted new assignment for which well trained. Quick wit veils serious mind.

♀ — Given opportunities to serve and still be paid or given recognitions for successful tasks fulfilled.

♂ — Escape from college pressures into a summer job. Initiator in the professional field.

? — Practical about setting goals.

♀ — Same as above.

⚹ — Married to a reputable person. Paired with a leader. Sign legal contract. Commitment to career precludes marriage.

⚜ — Denied practicing chosen profession.

♃ — Listed on probation by the professor. Teaches about the hidden or occult wisdom. Competency accepted.

♄ — Career communications blocked.

♅ — Received unexpected honors in the field of mathematics. Scientifically oriented mind.

♆ — Career record failed to show weaknesses. Qualifications are deceiving. Overestimate abilities. Original writings.

♇ — Desire to work for public good. Evaluation through career of service.

♃ — Birth of a girl child. Enjoys being around people. Gregarious tendencies.

⊕ — Lectures about mythology and archaeology. Limited authority. Superiors suspect activities and motives.

⚢ — Wishes for a military career and education. Energetic.

♈ — Known as a woman sufferage leader. Well qualified.

♃Ⅱ — Advance training or college degree for chosen field. An educator. Successful businessman.

⚛ — Need for times of solitude. Success must be well grounded.

⚕ — Curious about phenomena. Involved in odd practices. Other worldly. Interest in the occult.

♓ — Minister. Publicly employed as teacher of universal truth. Mouthing religious concepts. Founder of school. Dreamer.

⚴/A — Intercessor. Balanced schedule. Began elementary school. Art studio. Disciplined reactions. Professional person. Objectivity respected.

M — Well-known career woman. Successful profession in the art world. Capable worker.

A — Same as above.

☉ — Adored by co-workers and employees. Popular monarch. A gathering of professional people. The healthy body.

☽ — Simple contract or details made public.

☊ — Elected by popular mandate. Acclaimed by other group members. Chosen to this position.

♈ — Biography documented for public files. Intimacies revealed and life style widely known.

☿ — Self image as perpetual teacher. Explains details slowly and carefully to aid understanding. Clarity of mind and speech.

♀ — Received public award for accomplishments and loyalty to a superior and company.

♂ — Exhibits professionalism at all times. Calm under pressure. Time of an inauguration.

⚳ — Complacent. Born of a simple family. Loves the earth.

⚴ — Same as above.

⚵ — Platonic relationships with married women. Teaching or lecturing groups of housewives. Objective tutor.

⚶ — Disciplined artist. Childhood spent in training natural talents. Drilled thoroughly.

♃ — Good rapport with community regarding professional activities. Well received.

♄ — Reviewed job responsibilities. Resigned from work. Assumed added facets of career with or without promotion.

♅ — Professional astrologer or mathematician. Sharpened powers of observation used in portrait painting.

♆ — Ministerial association. Counseling drug addicts.

♇ — Applauded for job well done. Reknown. Suppressed feelings about kinfolk.

⯠ — United in battle. Home guard. Member of the reserves. From closely knit family group.

⯡ — Employing all classes of people. Career endeavors maligned. Working with roots of words and/or plants.

⯢ — Military accomplishments. Ancestors honored in battle.

⯣ — An able physician or politician. Concerned with justice.

⯤ — Member of the scientific community. Engineering organization.

⯥ — Completion of research. Digging into ancient history. Sabbatical. Looking from a different perspective.

⯦ — Joining a superior team. Ordination of priest. Within a frameword of inspiration provided by close associates.

⯧ — Translating theology into simple terms. Interpreting cosmic laws in diagram form. Use universal concepts daily.

☿/⊙	Uniformed man or woman. Bodily modesty. Prepared. Applied psychology. Inclined toward job change. Day of practical handiwork. Career satisfaction. Further instruction.

M — Realizing the need for further instruction or education to meet career demands. Successful. Peace of mind. Humble.

A — Approval and support of superior and associates.

⊙ — Same as above.

☽ — Adoration from the masses. Crowned a queen. Ultimate acceptance from peers. Ethical behavior.

☊ — Completely immune. One of a homogeneous group. Balanced.

♈ — Official representative. Authority publicly conferred. In an open classroom or training session.

☿ — Pleasant conversationalist. Good public relations person. Enables children to begin professional endeavors.

♀ — Creates in clay as a potter. Physically attractive. Sister working. Honors received by woman. Mathematical female.

♂ — Military officer. Good organizer. Convened meeting of dissidents.

? — Published a book about peasants in China. Land reformer. Birth of a writing or manuscript.

☿ — Same as above.

⚹ — Bought part interest in a horse with a friend who became a partner. Small business with family member. Treasurer.

↓ — Seclusion necessary for serious work and contemplation. Engaged in profession demanding much personal effort.

♃ — Tendency toward weight problems. Day of release from pain. Religious leader.

♄ — Quit vocational school. Job separates from power. Body suppressed by responsibility. Elder statesman. Aging wisely.

♅ — Original writer and lecturer. Professor of mathematics. Creative person. Astrologer.

♆ — Disappointed by military action. Idealistic solution to handling police pressures. Covers hurts by jokes.

♇ — Reverses teaching methods. Reevaluating purpose of mental development. Objective educator.

⚴ — Ceremony of religious commitment. Dedication to career. Vow of induction.

⊕ — Working with disabled or retarded persons.

⚵ — Involvement with military personnel. Capable and creative. Gives clear instructions or orders.

♈ — Hired by the major employer. Capable ruler. = Venus, an able woman in charge or queen as sovereign.

⚶ — Justice served. Acknowledged as a learned leader of chosen profession.

⚸ — Digging into ancient material. Sabbatical for profound research. Seeing job training from different perspective.

♋ — Excellent physical build aids in both good health and career advancement.

♓ — Recognized as a priest in own right. No longer an associate. Sincerely religious.

☿ / ☽	Working mother. Creative person. Practical mind. Protective. Channeling. Uniformed woman. Unusual outlet for emotions. Resumed working. The public feminist.

M — Began writing again. Put emotions into a physical task.

A — Counseling. Analyzed emotions of others. Determined but charming. Working family relationship.

☉ — Unusual outflow of body fluids. Sensitive to feelings of others. A practical leader.

☽ — Same as above.

☊ — Harmonious working association. Congenial. Enjoys work with women. Spread out but dealing with common purpose

♈ — News of a feminist rally. Suffragettes. Queen's proclamation.

☿ — A Safety Patrol mother. Request for legal protection. File clerk. Statements of women's equality.

♀ — Stands up for a mother's natural rights. Fortunate in the career. Catering. Happy at work.

♂ — Becomes a pacifist. Protective mate. Controls emotions by Oriental techniques. Hard, physical tasks. Nervous tension.

⚴ — Rolling bandages for hospital or military use. Working with health problems. Nutritional counseling. Seamstress.

⚳ — Same as above.

⚵ — Married to career woman. Mate interested in child care or ecology. Public health works. Controls emotions in public.

⚶ — Denied expected comforts of which profession usually merits. Not accepted by colleagues.

♃ — Finds contentment caring for foster retarded child. Accepts motherhood as a career.

♄ — Geneology. Difficult career transition. Successfully changed from silent to vocal film star.

♓ — Overdrafts. Extravagant. Quick mind. Glandular disorder creates lack of immunity to contagious diseases.

♅ — Drugs taken with food. Ingestion of poison by mistake.

♇ — Child of political marriage. Inherited mother's need for power. Plummeted into leadership at an early age.

♃ — Works in the public eye. Grows up with additional concerns. Inherits through the maternal side.

⊕ — Working mother. Abandoned for mother's career. Feels rejected in later years.

⚷ — Mother forced to seek employment. Terrible temper. Directed anger. Dream realized. Strongly confront challenges.

♈ — Innate vision leads beyond static understanding. Strongly creative. Follow's a woman's leadership. Owns a horse.

♊ — A mechanic. Traveler's aid helper.

♀ — Led the country through time of sorrow. Carried on in an emergency. Calmly efficient in dilemma.

△ — Warning the public of great danger. Inspired. Martial arts instructor.

♓ — A working medium. Fully ordained priest or minister.

| ☿/☋ | Library associations or groups. Handicraft guilds. Horse trainers. National Guardsmen. Business connection. |

M — Active in many organizations. Understands committee work. Familiar with group procedure.

A — Trained by a small, elite group. Served as a parliamentarian. Born into a military family.

⊙ — Staunch party supporter. Active participant in the campaign. Involved with groups or a mob.

☽ — Working in public affairs. Business procedure handled in front of witnesses.

☋ — Same as above.

♈ — Organized a group to live by her philosophies. Well-known. Rational woman.

☿ — Speaks distinctly. Delivers credible address or lecture. Receives congratulations.

♀ — Classified as a capable authoress. Associated with females.

♂ — Orchestrated well. Competent director or manager. Often overworked because of personal drive.

? — Shepherd of his or her own flock. Given own congregation or department to manage. Encourages patronage.

☿ — Same as above.

⚹ — Accident involved others. Responds only to selective programming. Frightened.

↓ — Body unable to make a complete recovery from injuries. An incomplete immune system.

♃ — Train horses for associate. United in a common cause. Expands cooperative ventures. Judges abilities.

♄ — Disciplined co-worker. Conservative on job. Liaison at work. Kept from study by older person. Left school.

♅ — Associated with an innovative person or a co-inventor.

♆ — Member of radio and TV corporation. Vivid imagination. Romantic fantasies written in story form.

♇ — Involved in shady business dealings. Get-rich quick idea.

— Attending marriage of business associate.

— Problems at work with the public. Opinionated because of past problems. Prosaic.

— Honorary member of military. Commissioned through the family connections. Uses others to get ahead.

— Manager of large group of people. Elected as chairman.

— Professor of mathematics or astronomy. Fine horse trainer.

— Persistent.

— Support from influential persons. Successful career. Associated with talented musicians. Powerful alliances.

— Ministerial association. Priestly orders. Monasteries.

♀ / ♈	Conference for workers. N.A.T.O. Peacemakers. Peace Corps. Patents. Catalogs. Began schooling or vocational training. Confers with others.

M — Interest in working with a group or organization.

A — Involved with relatives who make the news. Family oriented information. Invitation to teach or speak.

☉ — Main speaker. Keynote speech about vocations. Renown. Important stage performer. Remembered for job well done.

☽ — Emotional about project or services at work. Famous for efforts during a crusade.

☊ — Knowledgeable in chosen field.

♈ — Same as above.

☿ — Author of published books and articles. Professional tour lecturer. Textbooks.

♀ — Gives a pleasing public appearance when on duty. Achieved moderate success. Brought about peaceful solution.

♂ — Energies devoted to work area.

⚳ — Pictured as a militant type of person. Member of the Women's Army Corps.

⚥ — Same as above.

⚴ — Works with mate. Employed by spouse. Thorough researcher. Supported by husband or wife.

↓ — Wrecked own career. Drove self for recognition. Craved public acclaim for work.

♃ — Internationally known minister and counselor. Espouses public causes.

♄ — Follows strength. Bows to superior abilities. Patient worker and supporter.

♅ — Notoriety. Career related accident. Active in backing unpopular liberal causes.

♆ — Acknowledged as an excellent actress. Film award. Led large revivals. Remembered for religious activities.

♇ — Crusader. Recruited volunteers. Innovative. Would enjoy turning the world upside down.

⚴♀ — Received early promotions. Well liked by co-workers. Personable employee.

⊕ — Appears to be neurotic.

⚷ — Pushed into the public eye. Fulfillment in achievements.

♈ — Associates with accepted leaders, worldwide or locally.

♃ — Trained to function as member of a team of specialists.

⚇ — Overly serious about world affairs.

⚴ — Head of a department. Much favorable publicity. Forceful personality.

⚹ — Dedicated to improving national images. Evangelistic fervor. Shares personal inspiration with others.

Rationalizes shortcomings. Understands failures. Teaches.
Practical mode of expression. Intuitive mind. Nervous.
Professional mathematical examinations. Voice lessons.

M — Accepted new teaching position. Woman journalist. Shares knowledge of fundamentals and media.

A — Banking or financial institution. Information kept within the family or a close group of friends.

☉ — Drill instructor or coach. Charismatic natural leader. A natural mimic. Mathematics tutor.

☽ — Problems with child affect the career. Establishes a mood to build rapport with an audience.

☊ — Friendly with strangers. Fits into sales positions.

♈ — Professional actress. Endeavors are understood as a means of communicating with the public.

☿ — Same as above.

♀ — Enjoys speaking engagements. Artistic. Discreet in communications. Creates harmony. Pleasant voice. Study of colors.

♂ — Public speaking classes. Pink ransom note. Nervous tension arises out of overwork.

♃ — Practical mode of expression. Terse speech patterns. Accepted job programming data for friend's book.

♀ — Same as above.

♓ — Cautious spokesperson.

☊ — Memorizes data or information from master craftsman. Respects learned scholar. Apprenticeship. Loss of freedom.

♃ — Receives a well-earned degree.

♄ — Lack of support from co-workers. Separative thoughts. Lack of employment opportunities. Responsible intelligence.

♓ — Good athletic timing. Sense of rhythm. Strikes when the iron is hot. Unusual creative writing style.

♆ — Tape records meditations and mood music. Discusses personal endeavors as an individual link with mankind.

♇ — Learns and understands from failures.

♃ — Study and teaching principles of harmony. Reflexology. Beautifully modulated voice pattern.

♁ — Public lecture delayed by bad weather.

⚡ — Engineering principles. Plans the details of military training maneuvers.

♈ — Leadership training seminars. Chairing meetings.

♃♊ — Associated professionally with social elite. Minor success through artistic efforts.

♀ — Helped establish a new elementary school. Firm foundation for educational institution. Educational director.

♎ — Powerful incentive.

♓ — Religious ritual. Priest touched by the bishop. Teach spiritual development.

☿ / ♀	Pleasant co-worker. Social activity with fellow employees. Woman engineer. Synthesis of colors. Jeweler. High-fashion accessories. Loves a banker. Sympathetic.

M — Winner of multiple international awards for endeavors.

A — Partnership in jewelry manufacturing and distributing firm. Opened a fashionable dress shop.

☉ — Designed jewelry which was manufactured and sold. Crowned on abdication of mother. Half interest in race horse.

☽ — Financially conservative. Public enjoyed prosperity. Jobs were plentiful. = Aries, for female buyers.

☊ — Works well with women.

♈ — Received own assignment. Graduated. Wins professional opening. Striking physical beauty.

☿ — Forerunner. Trial model. Chatters about fellow employees. Commercial writing. Office parties. Clothes fasteners.

♀ — Same as above.

♂ — Army successful in keeping peace. Defense mechanism sound. Working advantages.

⚳ — Unassuming.

⚥ — Same as above.

⚴ — Regimented affections leads to being considered unresponsive. Difficulties in relationships.

⚶ — Obtuse toward mate. Replaced by new and improved model. Anti-feminist. No children. Retooled.

♃ — Money received from jewelry design. People take advantage. Valiant warrior.

♄ — To bide one's time. Health beginning to fail. Work in costume jewelry business. Long struggle for equality.

♅ — Endorsed unique ideology. Competitive. Clever. Strange sense of humor. Fluctuating glucose level in blood.

♆ — Professional training overseas. Made office a retreat. Withdrawn from work environment. Photographer. Reclusive.

♇ — Professional position transformed by undercover act. Watergate. Psychological problems from inability to blend natures.

⚵ — Considers the family an important part of play and work time.

⚷ — Rebel. Profound research on metabolism.

⚸ — Head of movie studio wardrobe department. Rapid expansion. Apparent prosperity.

⚯ — Elevated to a position of some authority in one's field.

⚼ — Cultured. Affectionate in a reserved way. Enjoys good companionship.

⚨ — Election to office delayed. Promotion withheld.

⚺ — Powerful career woman. Mathematical genius for sister. Imposing physical appearance.

⚹ — Inspired by the music in religious services. Likes pipe organs.

☿ / ♂	Diligent worker. Hazardous use of energy. Connecting link. Haste makes waste. Energetic employee. Beginning of a career. Ineffectual because of overzealousness.

M — Goal oriented. Respects accomplishments. Overconfident.

A — Appears frail for the appointed task. Working on a team. Member of group endeavor.

☉ — Self-defeating. Not using one's full potential. Growth hindered. Erratic spurts.

☽ — Upset about salary. Spasmodic work habits. Agreement reached. Concerned with working conditions.

☊ — Employment agency. Labor representative.

♈ — Woman trying to fill a man's shoes. To drive self beyond physical endurance. Blunders.

☿ — Vocational or trade school training. Simple writer. News of lover. Enthusiastic student.

♀ — Indulgent. Encourages erratic work habits in others. A certain lack of discipline.

♂ — Same as above.

⚵ — Desire to be useful. Implementing plans to adopt or deliver a child. Put others before her career advancement.

⚶ — Same as above.

⚴ — Final agreement on terms of contract. The hunt. Form of equestrian jumping.

⚷ — Loss of job. Farsighted in face of multiple difficulties. Overzealous.

♃ — Joyous events in professional life. To work with one's own sons. Fortunate employee.

♄ — Overworked. Fatigue causes inefficiency. Inflammation and infection of the bone marrow.

⛢ — Accident prone. Minor mechanical mishaps. Combatant. A radical.

♆ — Female prison chaplain. Searcher for the truth. Struggle through a maze. Fighting deceptions.

♇ — Alchemist. Changes careers at midlife.

⚵ — Married to working partner. Family business. Aware of traditions. Main support of the family.

⊕ — Dirty work. Digging through accumulated debris.

⚸ — Diligent crusader. Leadership potential developed gradually.

♈ — Military or civil service career.

⚴ — Accountant. Conferring a professional degree. Graduate. Continuing study. Fellowship.

⚥ — Fierce determination. Bad working conditions.

♌ — Analytical.

⚹ — Unable to discriminate. Confused about reality. Torn between the spiritual and material worlds.

♀/⚻	Social standards of the day. Family business. Working wife. Co-operative husband and spouse. Practical legal action. Clairvoyance.

M — Public declaration of purpose. Tightly structured. Official. Mind control. Restricted from releasing fully. High IQ.

A — Snobbish. Ancestor devotion. Foolish false pride. Brags about family achievements.

⊙ — Accepted financial obligations. Hour of witnessing a signature. Graduation day.

☽ — Receiving public compliments.

♌ — Keeps a certain distance from co-workers. Formal approach in groups. Appreciates traditional rituals.

♈ — Torn membranes. Sexual experience exposed in public. Rejection by mate known by all. Convenient alliance.

☿ — Sharp words that wound feelings. Swift jabs with either hands or tongue.

♀ — Women working together without spouse. Crises from lack of affection in relationships.

♂ — Compatible marriage or partnership of equally talented persons.

? — Word connotations important. Blends marriage and career. Female partnership.

♀ — Same as above.

⚻ — Same as above.

↓ — Denies marriage. Uptight on the job. Precise. Working woman sacrifices relationships.

♃ — Family enterprise grew. Spouses worked hard together. Shared major decisions with another.

♄ — Loss of employment because of social peer action. Mate's illness. Assumes the chores and responsibilities of another.

♆ — Treason. Following a firmly established government protocol. Unique actions.

♅ — **Unrealistic** about time. Installation. Signed by a film company.

♀ — Disruptive with co-workers. Psychic experiences. Fanatic about conforming to personal concepts.

♃ — Supportive of home and family.

⊄ — Deprived by family business. Succored the dying. Works one's way out of poverty. The last rites. Slum work.

⚷ — Socially acceptable. Regal appearance. Imposing office.

♈ — Emotionally and legally bound to domineering people. A spouse from the social register.

♃Ⅱ — Trained in homemaking and herbal remedies. Made a good marriage.

♀ — Ostracized because of moralistic attitude. Prudish.

△ — Forced to conclude a business transaction. Pushed into signing a contract.

⚹ — Ordination of priest or minister. Idealizes the concept of combined career and marriage.

60

Fastidious. Dedicated worker. Martyr complex. Psychic.
Failure of a business. A liberal feminist crusader.

M — The need for balance. Misunderstood ambitions.

A — Work around fussy relatives. Standing alone for personal beliefs. Persistent efforts exerted.

☉ — One who has publicly taken monastic vows. A truly dedicated person. Preference for men.

☽ — Haertbroken by demands. Family takes precedence over career. Segregated for expression of beliefs. Grief-striken mother.

☊ — Family response upsets and affects work habits.

♈ — Honored for professional dedication. Strenuous service to others. Destined for high purpose.

☿ — Voices frustration about sacrifices. Dislike of crowded rooms or air waves. Dedication speech.

♀ — Attractive representative. Broken blood vessels. Survivor of twins. Adopted girl. A dandy. Unusual uniforms.

♂ — Dedicated worker. Irritated by financial difficulties. Innate mathematical and business acumen. Earnest.

? — Prompt and adequate medical attention. Cares for minority faction. Industrial. Passive resistance.

♀ — Same as above.

✝ — Denied joys of wedded bliss. Conformed to Puritan ideals. Critical of credit economy. Equates work and virtue.

↓ — Same as above.

♃ — Bred horses for sale and training. Incorporated. Benefactor died.

♄ — Damaged perception. Sensual deficiency. Communication is hampered by learning process.

♆ — Investigates time spans. Explosive. Looks at the past through use of legends and myths.

♆ — Unrealistic zeal for achievements. Thwarted in advancement. Career in photography or films.

♀ — Purges through dedication to career. Religious concept of personal importance.

♃♀ — Denied the warmth and generosity of normal relationships.

⊕ — Laboriously digs up all the facts before presenting a proposal. Works with disadvantaged persons after hours.

⚡ — Zealously militant.

♈ — Frustrated by being denied a position of authority. In league with the cemetery caretakers.

♃Ⅱ — Capable of leadership. Temporary work with educators. Denied college education or degree.

⊕ — Deprived and punished by primitive working conditions. Servile. Accepts lesser position in troubled time.

△ — An understanding of higher powers. Respectful.

♓ — Father takes part in ordination service. Knighted.

61

☿ / ♃	Successful in career endeavors. School textbook editor. Minister. Profitable employment. Promotion. Statesman. Elevated to high offices. Woman athlete.

M — Personal satisfaction derived from professional work or vocation. Grading or evaluating time.

A — Healthy and contented environment.

☉ — Scholarly. Adhered to strict religious teachings. Solemn. Achieved success, even to becoming President.

☽ — Balanced family and career evenly. Contract offer accepted. Radio script selected. Carried out expansion. Economics.

☊ — Fortunate connections at work. Being around lucky co-workers. Associated with ministers.

♈ — General economic upturn.

☿ — Published writings. Evangelist. Congratulations received. Brother a strict disciplinarian.

♀ — Earned money creating ceramics. Demonstrates fine points of great works of art. Sweater girl. Uses visual aids.

♂ — Accepted a new job. Well-informed for vocational requirements. Skilled worker.

♁ — Licensed minister serving as institutional chaplain. Foster parent. Associated with orphanage.

♀ — Same as above.

⚸ — Researching details for article or lecture to be published. Formal commencement ceremony. Ordination of minister.

⚷ — Ambitions nipped in the bud. Forced to accept loss of fame. Resigned from office because of convictions.

♃ — Same as above.

♄ — Impracticalities frowned upon. Taught to handle money in the right way at an early age.

♓ — Disruptive. Textbook selection committee member. Excitement mounting. Caused stir in meeting.

♆ — Deceived by business partner. Problems with joint finance. Monetary goals unrealistic. Misjudged abilities.

♇ — Forced to close because of overexpansion.

⚵ — Happily married to accountant. Member of harmonious family. Involved in large business venture.

⊕ — Loss of financial support. Business cash flow problems. Weight problem. Periods of suppression of expression.

⚶ — Ability to pour energy into a given project.

♈ — Capable handling of complicated task. Overcome a government crisis.

♃Ⅱ — Vocational training. Mechanical or mathematical understanding. Enjoys puzzles and quizzes.

⚴ — One of the elite. A special scholar among the clergy or rabbinical students. Well grounded in subjects.

⚺ — Approaches ventures with self-confidence.

⚻ — Died with dignity. Brings an assurance to conferences.

♀/♄	Advisor or counselor. Employer. Loss of employment. Depleted body. Lenient with self. Passed over at promotion time. Disappointing job transfer. Separations.

M — Learning to understand failures and setbacks.

A — Isolated from relatives. Employed in a far country or away from home. Absence of parental training.

☉ — Reputation for excellence. Must become a role model for others. Forced to toil harder than co-workers.

☽ — Duty separates from mother's comfort. Slave trade began. Well-regulated schedule. Enslaved by demands. Task accepted.

☊ — Associated with those who choose heavy labor. Accepted the burdens of public office. Presented to many people.

♈ — Slow to become accepted as capable. Unwilling to project.

☿ — Unable to fully express personal knowledge at testing.

♀ — Possible loss of love and respect. Normal defenses set aside. Vulnerable period.

♂ — Frustrated efforts. Responsible and hard working. Manager. Agitated leader. Brave in face of adversity.

? — Accepts and counters the restrictions of birth.

♀ — Same as above.

⚴ — Through illness or loss of a mate becomes very involved in a vocation. Speak softly and carry a big stick.

⚳ — A life of hard work and perseverance.

♃ — Did not received the expected holiday bonus. Aided by the engineering contracts.

♄ — Same as above.

♅ — Unexpectedly not employed. Sick leave for surgical recovery. Erratic working hours.

♆ — Divorce changed financial status. Idealistic about foreign people. Mental arrogance confuses others.

♇ — Allows self to feel victimized. Tendency to submit to the wishes of autocratic people.

♅ — Separated from relatives because of duty.

⊕ — Dismissed for reasons of psychological instability.

⚵ — Fired quite suddenly and firmly.

⚶ — Employment terminated by authorities. Forced into retirement. Tax problems.

⚷ — Graduation. Installation. Leaving for a higher position.

⚸ — Killed on the job. Guilty of gross neglect. Death or injury from mistakes in judgment. Reputation marred.

⚺ — Non-academic. Severe and unexplained breakdown of the body's immune system.

⚻ — Separation from social and religious traditions of one's childhood. Solemn installation or ceremony.

Programming computers. Calculated risks. Piloting. Loopholes. Excitement in knowledge. Traveled in search of an education. Career peaks and ebbs. Notoriety. Calculations.

M — Struggled against established authority in her field.

A — Cooperative relatives. Parents who encouraged development of unusual talent. Stimulating environment.

⊙ — Remarkable memory. Suddenly achieved lasting fame. Zany script brought super-star status. Energetic.

☽ — Designed occult pendant for public usage. Mother of the Pentacostal Holiness movement. Fosters strange ideologies.

☊ — Abstract plans revealed for public scrutiny.

♈ — Erratic disruption of ties. Body suddenly loses its ability to control spread of disease.

☿ — Professor. Lectures. Author. Humanitarian journalist.

♀ — Capricious pathway to chosen field. Aspiring actress. Sporatic bookings and parts for entertainer.

♂ — Working astrologer. Profitably pioneering in a new project.

♃ — Unable to maintain a job for any length of time. Fitful appetites. Spasms of the upper intestine.

♀ — Same as above.

⚥ — Dubious powers to act through another person. Few rights.

↓ — Popularity swung from unprecedented high to unexpected low. Trapped by own actions. Resignation suddenly requested.

♃ — Success and power given quickly and unexpectedly.

♄ — Problems of timing brought about on the job. Day versus night tempo. Frequent change of shifts. Lose a venture.

♓ — Same as above.

♅ — Famous television star. Sudden losses of memory. Sense of smell obscured.

♀ — Unplanned birth. Surprise the public with unusual procedures.

♃ — Sudden career connections revealed. Unpredictable co-workers. Electrical corporation. Family TV station.

⊕ — Radioactive minerals. Unpleasant fires.

⚡ — Impulsive. Drastic action. Retaliation for either real or imagined wrongs.

⚚ — Irregular hours of leadership training. = Cupido, title hereditary.

♃♊ — Successful athlete.

⚥ — Loss of spontaneity.

⚴ — Pilot of private or commercial aircraft. Study and understanding of aerodynamics.

⚹ — Professor of astrology and esoteric sciences. Trained to manipulate instruments by touch alone. Inspired.

☿ / ♆	Uncertain about responsibilities. Dream analysis. Artist. Disillusionment on job. Organist in church. Curious reasons for working. Poetic.

M — Overly sensitive to criticism. Perfectionist. One who can be a compulsive worker at times.

A — Involved in paramedic group. Investigating team.

☉ — Vulnerable body. Self-analyst. Health affected by atmospheric conditions. One behind the apparent authority. Self error.

☽ — Cruel tendencies hidden beneath passive exterior. Disillusioned. Emotionally damaged by maternal objectivity.

☊ — Interrupted career in theater. Inconsistent.

♈ — Noteworthy new healing procedure. Publicized for role in promoting psychic phenomena.

☿ — Work in pediatrics. Expressing personal opinion. Restraint in answering questions. Uneasy.

♀ — Content amidst the confusion. Greeted with rapture before the problem was aired. Naive.

♂ — Inbalance of adrenaline affects hormone production. Hapless future outlook. Ambition denied by male. Untimely end.

♀ — Using folk medicine or herbal remedies.

♀ — Same as above.

♃ — Caught short by being unprepared. Hardships from lack of work. Held back by need for training and understanding. Hungry.

↓ — Periodic stoppages in career for birth and raising of children. Glandular malfunction of the lymph system.

♃ — Diplomatic immunity.

♄ — Disappointed convention delegate. Separative action taken out of faith in certain principles.

♅ — Resigned from pr fessional position without obvious reason. Unplanned changes confuse career direction.

♆ — Same as above.

♇ — Growth and regeneration through struggle to find a suitable vocation. Tried to revise administrative structure.

♃♀ — Cooperating with the ministerial association for charity.

♀ — Delayed decision caused fatality. Pilot's uncertainty resulted in aircraft plummeting to earth.

⚹ — Disillusioned about supposed organizational ability. Dreams of power. Delusions of grandeur. Escapes daily drudgery.

♈ — Diplomatic or government counselor. Important film star.

♃♊ — Exchange of currency for several countries. Fluctuations.

♀ — Professional photographer, works in the dark room.

⚹ — Sent overseas for training. Intimidated. Propelled into rapid advancement before readied.

♓ — Achievement of greatest dream. Fair-minded.

☿/♇	Upheavals in career. Mental anguish. Dictatorial attitude. Tried to uncover hidden patterns of life. Intense teaching of esoteric knowledge. Digging.

M — Fast reactions. Capable of rapid changes.

A — Provides for others. Unselfish. Discussed worldwide trans-formations. A bridge. Attempted reconciliations.

☉ — Creative individual who understands public appeal. Psycholog-ical control by demanding female.

☽ — Feeling abandoned.

☊ — Undercover connections. Private liaison.

♈ — Falsify documents. Inaccurate calculations.

☿ — New methods of farming introduced. Tremendous changes brought about by use of slaves or admirers. Hypnotic or persuasive.

♀ — Love for a co-worker in group endeavors.

♂ — Working for brother. Lost job in divorce. Attacking hidden problems. Possible controversy. Alarmed by trends.

⚴ — Provided fostering and nurturing environment for research. Not adverse to getting dirty or digging in the soil.

⚳ — Same as above.

⚵ — Mate changes career plans. Wife notified of death of her husband in work-related accident.

⚶ — Completely immersed in a project or problem. Struggled vainly to clear disgrace from career record.

♃ — Praised for expose. Involved in extensive manhunt. Uncover-ed spy ring. Searched deeply in recesses of the mind.

♄ — Separated from associates and family. Leads students from one place to another. Brings order out of chaos.

♅ — Psychomotor irregularities. Release of energies. Sporadic.

♆ — Hypnotherapist. Psychologist. Compelling manner. Atheist.

♇ — Same as above.

⚷ — Taken into the family. Reception following ceremony.

⊕ — Sociologist who counsels distrubed people.

⚸ — Uses a lot of energy working on small projects.

♈ — Needs a strong father image to follow.

♃Ⅱ — Selected by popular approval. Forceful leader. Experienced instructor or lecturer.

⚼ — Betrayed. Proceeds in face of public disapproval.

⚴ — Strong temptation to advance by irregular methods. Pluto-crat. Overbearing co-worker. Mighty aspirations.

⚹ — Career upheaval due to traumatic emotional experience.

66

⚴ / ♃♀ — Good defenses. Promoted. Winner. Family ties. Responsible. Awards. Tests come from career demands. An achiever.

M — Business revision and expansion.

A — Rapid recovery of companions. Promoted to leader.

☉ — A superior body immunity system.

☽ — Popular manager or supervisor. Liked by co-workers and employees.

☊ — Consolidation. Business conglomerate. Alliance of persons of differing cultures. Corporate enterprise.

♈ — Publicly involved in popular issues. Wide media exposure. Business achievements acknowledged.

☿ — Shorthand. Executive secretary. Children's toy manufacturer. Editing company newsletter.

♀ — Party to celebrate promotion.

♂ — Procedures established for personnel. Industrial company. Fever accompanying viral illness.

⚳ — Janitorial service. Care of the family. Maternal attitude. Small investor in local businesses.

⚴ — Same as above.

⚵ — Healthy and easy natural childbirth. Congenial mate.

⚶ — Family tragedy. Separated from loved ones. Periodic.

♃ — Brings cheer to associates. Appreciated. Welcome guest. Advantages to alliance.

♄ — Students became like his children. Work was his family. Serious companion. Unfortunate business association.

♅ — Capable of fanatic attachments to family members.

♆ — The working woman who is a bad parent. Incorporated the dreams of an entire nation.

♇ — Completed book about need for public changes. Sacrificed self desires for sibling needs.

♃♀ — Same as above.

⊕ — Missed appointment because of family illness. Mother remained home to nurse sick child. Fulfillment delayed.

⚷ — Family forced apart by professional demands. Powerful corporation. Wife and children loyal during campaigns.

⚸ — Elected to important government office. Investiture of high responsibility.

♃♊ — Community leader. Raised funds for public causes. Patron of the arts.

⛢ — Career commitments delayed marriage.

⚹ — Serving higher power on a professional basis. Minister.

♓ — Hopeless search for group of like interests.

<table>
<tr><td>☿/⊕</td><td>Unemployed. Handicapped worker. Works by observing socio-logical changes. Chronic illness.</td></tr>
</table>

M — Concerned about lack of job opportunities. Discouraged.

A — Joined small association involved in social concerns.

☉ — Deserted or orphaned early in life. Correcting prior injustices to all peoples. Strangely arresting.

☽ — Unable to function in normal social situation. Hidden tendencies toward periodic violence. Sensitive to restraint.

☊ — Vocational counseling seminar. Conflicts within a group.

♈ — Lack of jobs. A recession period. Depressing neighborhood.

☿ — Crime reporter for newspaper. Epidemic of childhood diseases.

♀ — Making cheap candy. Using a substitute to cut expenses. Eat like a glutton. Mundane jobs for women.

♂ — Banished during war or struggles. Occupied homeland. Substitute for another in time of stress.

⚵ — Lived in poverty because of job deficiency. Withheld many popular foodstuffs.

⚴ — Same as above.

⚸ — Denying marriage and family for sake of career. Concerned with social welfare of the poor and lonely.

⚳ — Shudder at vulgarity. Social worker who fought for beliefs. Devoted to an unpopular cause.

♃ — Expectations not realized. Liver disease or damage.

♄ — Work doubly hard for any benefits. Concerns with continuation. Medicated for tooth extraction. Concentrate on basic wisdom.

⛢ — Fighting the atrocities of war. Rectal surgery. Cleaning up a long-standing health problem.

♆ — Alcoholic parent. Author of escapist stories.

♇ — Recommendations from employers vary. Analyze problems.

⚴♀ — Breakup of family unity. Work out of necessity. Not career oriented. Impoverished. Loss of inheritance or credibility.

⊕ — Same as above.

⚶ — Forced to work. Employed for survival.

♈ — Prison reform.

♃⚷ — Research on degenerative diseases. Discordant music.

⚕ — Strong form achieved by seeing career as a miniature reflection of contemporary culture as well as recording of present.

⚴ — Forced to work in dismal surroundings. Struck by lightning. Old house to be remodeled.

♓ — Visions of past glories.

| ☿/♐ | Focused career drive. Campaign for public office. Driven in professional endeavors. Civil engineer in military service. Archery. Mentally controlled. |

M — Creative endeavors. Disciplined employee. Well trained.

A — From a military family.

☉ — Fault of native. Bodily harm from being obstinate. Mathematics instructor or tutor. Revolutionary.

☽ — Upset about superior on job. Career advancement controlled by public opinion. Works for sales commission.

☊ — Conflict of interests. Military maneuvers.

♈ — News of achievements.

☿ — Objective editor and writer. Thorough documentation. Refer.

♀ — Works with domineering females. Pleasant but firm boss.

♂ — Foot soldier. Able mechanic.

⚴ — Prolonged periods of concentration. Worker who appreciates intense study habits.

⚶ — Same as above.

⚷ — Disciplined work habits. Chronicles past battles.

⚳ — Complete commitment to career.

♃ — Magnetic personality. Undaunted worker or employee. Energizes co-workers or persons in the vicinity.

♄ — Ambitions thwarted. Defeated for high office. Delayed in being nominated for desired position.

♅ — Unusual venting of energies. Innovative study or project. Domineering co-worker.

♆ — Minister. Led by the spirit. Inspired profession. Caution.

♇ — Resolves problems in a unique manner.

⚵ — Prolific worker. Concerned with family relations or marriage counseling.

⚻ — Applies understanding to disorder. Steadily builds up resistance to being affected by filth or rejection.

⚸ — Same as above.

⚹ — Cosmogenesis. Studies the original theories. Primordial man. Genesis interpretation.

♃♊ — Professional certification. Bar exam.

⚼ — Barbed wire fence. Boot spurs. Unsolicited sexual approach in the office environment.

⚺ — Suffers the horrors of war. Live through tremendous trials.

⚷ — Reveals simple truths. Establishes tranquil setting through use of vocal cadence. Seeks other planes of existence.

♀/♇	President or Chairman of the Board. Bishop. Famous. To have a personal business or establish a company. Legal authority. Judged. Natural leader or tycoon.

M — Strong leadership. Charming, magnetic personality. Leads.

A — Self-centered.

⊙ — Expert in given field of endeavor. Prominent. To be given responsibility.

☽ — A hired public official. Appointed.

☊ — Associated with superiors. Chosen to represent peers.

♈ — News of important personages. Popular biography. Intervention.

☿ — Wrote a book about hyperactive children. Nutritional research and writings. Published papers about nutritional findings.

♀ — Won the judge to her point of view.

♂ — Energetic. Innovative. Able to initiate action.

♁ — Government intelligence agent. Calm.

☿ — Same as above.

⚥ — Challenge of power in relationships.

☟ — Declined to seek high office. Sacrificed personal desires for harmony of corporation or political party.

♃ — Built up a personal corporation.

♄ — Enslaved. Held captive. Under power of stronger person.

♓ — Bonus. Labors over terms of report. Good at displaying merchandise to capture attention. Concise manner of thinking.

♅ — Chances for elevation disappeared. An impossible situation.

♀ — Major upheavals in leadership criteria. Heir to throne disposed. Extremely disappointed. Loss of trust.

♃ — Numbered among the leaders in chosen profession. Winner of many awards of merit.

♁ — Working for legislative reform. Lobbying. Attempts to rectify wrongs in the world. Humanitarian concerns.

⚸ — Energizes worldwide organization.

♈ — Same as above.

♃ — Trained for position. Promotion. Boss.

♀ — Ostracized. Passed over for promotion. McCarthyism. Henpecked. Fired. Loss of employment.

♂ — Great energies. Vivacious worker.

♓ — Guardian of spiritual laws. Clairvoyant.

☿ / ♃♊	Professional training. Brillant mind. Dean of a college. Accredited or qualified teacher. Renown authority. Engineering. Public credence.

M — Profoundly influenced by contemporaries.

A — Perpetual student. Scholarship. Associates with company or school personnel. Clean-cut appearance.

☉ — Competent college graduate. Professionalism.

☽ — Receiving public honors.

♎ — Fingers on the "pulse of the nation." Rapid typist.

♈ — Achieved public stardom. Acknowledged expert. Gains respect of colleagues. College professor.

☿ — Study for professional accreditation. Child prodigy. Spokesman for large corporation or group.

♀ — Able to look at greater concepts versus prevailing theories.

♂ — Spends hours on his feet. Qualified by on-the-job training.

? — Compassionate but calm parent. Working grandmother.

☿ — Same as above.

✳ — Rebels at constant exposure. Professional elite.

↓ — Deeply religious.

♃ — Relief after completing complicated technical work. Award.

♄ — Training not fully used. Trust lawyer.

♆ — Research into the unorthodox. Well trained in metaphysics.

♅ — Travel overseas to study for career.

♇ — Trained on the job. Practical experience through change.

♃ — On friendly terms with world leaders because of political office. Liaison between various authorities.

♁ — Historical winning period. Serves faithfully through a time of great deprivation and distress.

⚹ — Financial backing.

⇡ — Crowned or installed as an acknowledged authority. Promoted. Highly elevated in professional field. Inaugurated.

♃♊ — Same as above.

⚷ — Drudgery. Wasting energy and talents in an unrewarding capacity. Unappreciated.

△ — Forced into a position of authority. Chosen for exceptional accomplishments. Appointed. Capable bookkeeper.

⚸ — Visualizes self as an important figure. Always involved with those in positions of authority.

71

Defense against change. Impaired defense mechanism. Invalid vaccination. Seriously ill. Body immunity problems. Walls.

M — Calm in decision making. Not driven by ambition. Commodities market.

A — Uprooted from native land and family at an early age. Must remake own defense or support system.

☉ — Looked up to. Shared difficulties with countrymen. Health conditions stabilize. Mineral study.

☽ — Patience rewarded. Period of training successfully completed. Grieving for loss of mother or parental figure.

☊ — Symbol of freedom won through effort.

♈ — Real estate sale recorded.

☿ — A normally quiet person. Subtle sense of humor. Swears by a solemn oath.

♀ — A woman alone against time-honored customs.

♂ — Outburst of suppressed rage. Righteous indignation.

⚲ — Sheltered from unpleasantness.

⚲ — Same as above.

⚵ — Feelings of worthlessness because of spouse's career. Hard work to support family. Inured against peer criticism.

⚶ — Counters professional criticism by increased dedication to project at hand. Study origins of society.

♃ — Eventual fulfillment. Poignant.

♄ — Buried by heavy responsibilities. Susceptible to infection.

⚷ — Impaired circulation. Hemp rope. Constricts flow of blood. Mind absorbs and stores whatever is observed.

♆ — Possible nervous seizures. An emotional time.

♇ — Fanatic about changes. Subversive. Disruptive actions are concealed from co-workers. Adamant about status quo.

⚴ — Family refused to accept inability to carry out assignment.

⚳ — Lack of immunity to certain diseases. Researcher. Very little physical recuperative power.

⚸ — Many hours of hard labor restoring old home.

♈ — Destruction of barriers against voting rights.

⚵ — Blocked endocrine flow. Life forces vacillating and dying. Corporate failure. Embezzlement.

⚚ — Same as above.

⚺ — Fame and power delayed. Native skills developed through instruction. Given an assignment.

♓ — Deeply religious. Overcomes crises with abiding faith.

☿ ⁄ ♀ ⚴	Self motivation. Taught religious practices. Vigorous individual. Powerful mind. Controlled by outside forces. Forced into job by economic circumstances. Strength.

M — Self-confidence.

A — Underdeveloped charisma. Gives constructive criticism.

☉ — Determined to have own way. Focused personality. Determined.

☽ — Inspired public speaker. Civic theater performer.

♌ — Accepted job offer with important company.

♈ — Placed in an enviable position. General self-confidence.

☿ — X-ray technician. Athletic contestant. Speaks with sense of authority and purpose. Loud-mouthed troublemaker.

♀ — Romance writer. Objective and analytical about love.

♂ — Exposed to depravities of war. Forced to leave homeland. Works for private ideals.

⚶ — Simple people involved. Explains great events in terms of daily life. Accidently caught up in world crisis.

⚳ — Same as above.

⚵ — Strong pressure to achieve.

☋ — Concerned with funeral rituals.

♃ — Chosen out-of-the-blue for preferred job. Screen test miracle for future star. Lucky choice.

♄ — Ambitions influenced by father. Allowed to succeed slowly. Hindered in his advancement.

♅ — Startling discoveries revealed.

♆ — Unseen resources. Renown spiritual leader.

♇ — Self-made crusader.

⚵ — Loyalty. Faith in company of superiors justified.

♼ — Some hardships taken up purposefully. Carrying one's own cross. Committed to strict and primitive beliefs.

⚷ — Chosen by sudden, direct decision. Headed upward in career.

♈ — President of company came to investigate charges against him.

⚚ — Awarded a degree of fine arts. Achieves success in profession.

⚸ — Forced to deal objectively with death.

⚴ — Same as above.

⚹ — Intuitive. Brillantly lighted surface or office.

☿ / ⯑	Professional medium or spiritualist. Uses hunches or intuition in all dealings. Imaginative. Gambles at times.

M — Moderator of tests or examinations.

A — At least one minister in the family.

☉ — Standard bearer or cause. Rising above criticism. Refuses to lower principles to expedite plans.

☽ — Has a great deal of faith. Mother interested in mysticism.

☊ — Publicly accepted as professional metaphysician.

♈ — Life in the proverbial fishbowl.

☿ — Beginning trance development. Religious fanatic.

♀ — Small, but powerful.

♂ — Imaginative author.

⚳ — Showed proficiency on various instruments at an early age. Forever childlike. Born with pure vocal tones.

⚵ — Same as above.

⚴ — Married to a sensitive minister or counselor.

↓ — Dedicated researcher. Chaste.

♃ — Good judge of character.

♄ — History teacher or researcher.

♅ — Unusually creative author. Great empathy with all types of situations.

♆ — Clouds hindered perception. Technical errors uncovered. Investigation showed obscure weakness in electrical circuit.

♇ — Forced to abandon meaningful work. Tragedy. Drastic changes in goals. Loss of immediate superior.

⚷ — Strong family ties.

⊕ — Struggling to regain childhood faith.

⚶ — Able to pay heed to intuition. Learned to focus emotions at an early age.

⯓ — Wrote about world affairs. Inspired by international events. Successful.

⚼ — Kept high ideals throughout career. Respected by colleagues. Exceptional musician.

⚸ — Senses time for ecumenical movement in organized religions. Intellectual insight. Wisdom from long periods of study.

⚹ — Capable professional obsessed by desire to succeed. Religious vocation.

⯒ — Same as above.

⚧/M	Jealousy. Propriety. Personal opinion about legal partner. Marital concerns. Desire for social acceptance. Pettiness. Shrewd. Fidelity. Marriage finances become public.

M — Same as above.

A — Striking appearance. Dresses with distinctive flair.

☉ — Born to the social elite in one's environment. To upstage another. Condescending attitude. Good carriage. Beauty.

☽ — Concern for propriety. Public appearances. Mother is jealous of one's mate.

☊ — Restrictive in relationships. Requires strict observance of protocol at all times.

♈ — Publicly announced as a professional person.

☿ — Clipped, brusque speech. Enjoys appropriate ceremonies. Prone to anxiety about details.

♀ — Delightful career connection. Happily married to co-worker. Pleasant and dignified professional woman.

♂ — Works for social acceptance. Uptight about reputation. A Junior League volunteer.

? — Detached. Nurse who observes all the regulations.

⚨ — Defends spouse's reputation.

⚧ — Same as above.

⚷ — Talk with mate canceled. Denied one's hereditary social position. Takes odd jobs to support family.

♃ — Session with the Dean over grade probation. Life channeled into fruitful but narrow course.

♄ — Mentally and emotionally depressed. Thoughts of a divorce or separation.

♅ — Public success and excitement with partner.

♆ — Dreams of an ideal mate. Disillusioned by marriage. Opinions clouded by personal insecurities.

♇ — Purged of environmental and ancestral patterns for inner growth and development.

⚳ — Married couple shared political views.

⚴ — Research of social customs and traditions, including taboos.

⚵ — Civic-minded citizen or soldier.

⚶ — Adopts a superior attitude when defending one's beliefs. Certified by the state or legal authority.

⚷⚸ — Studying for credentials. Moment of certification. Needs reassurance. Warranty.

⚘ — Steadfast support from well-known relative.

⚸ — Powerful need to be free of bonds of protocol.

♓ — Time of religious ceremonies. A proper church wedding.

75

⚷ ╱ A	Confrontation with in-laws. Socially prominent. Formal wedding chapel. Intimate meetings with mate. Formal dinner. Grand opening of store. Famous friends.

M — Clever but retiring personality.

A — Same as above.

☉ — Modest about the body. Elegant and stately in appearance. Stylish dress.

☽ — Cosigner of legal papers, in front of witness.

♋ — Socially correct. Pleasant interludes in life. Enjoying social pleasantries. Entertaining personality.

♈ — Made a good impression on the general public. Congregation pledged themselves as well.

☿ — Concerned with peer approval. Cautious speaker. Stutters.

♀ — Affectionate mate. Pleasant thoughts of marriage. Greed.

♂ — Fight with husband or wife. Possessive spouse.

⚵ — Herbal remedies for healing disease.

⚶ — Careful budgeting of monies or time. Ideas shared by marriage partners. Good husbandman.

⚷ — Same as above.

☊ — Deliberately seeks confrontations. Shows disdain for accepted forms of behavior. Ignores objections.

♃ — Wealthy and properly dressed. Elaborate formal parties. Gains approval of peers.

♄ — Dislikes use of cosmetics.

♅ — Shocked by her family. Tried to escape traditions of upbringing. Unorthodox behavior. Creative.

♆ — Loosens legal bonds. Pretends to ignore normal exchange of courtesies. Easily deceived by flattery.

♇ — To divide into various components. Separate family members from each other.

⚴ — Family celebration such as birthday or anniversary party. Strict relatives. Reacts against disciplined childhood.

⊕ — Protective of family and loved ones. Retains the homestead. Mourns the loss of family customs.

⚸ — Others see mate as being powerful. Destiny of leadership for husband or wife. Under pressure from others.

⚳ — Married to a ruler. Official mating. Feels marriage is divinely inspired. Partner chosen by parents or authority.

⚵ — Office parties. Married into a college community. Attend the Dean's tea.

⚱ — Community property laws.

⚼ — Selective about friends and acquaintances. Married into a powerful family.

⚹ — Conservative religious affiliations.

76

⚴/☉	Bridegroom. Day of the wedding or other ceremony. Men in formal clothing. Sarcastic. Resentful. Socially prominent host. Inauguration. Physical decoration for peer approval.

M — Dresses in accord with upper-class established norms. Fits conservative social pattern.

A — Sees himself or herself as a respected member of the community regardless of the circumstances.

☉ — Same as above.

☽ — Merry widow. Enjoys the company of women. Leader of social clique. Contained emotions.

☊ — Dependable clubwoman. Political volunteer. A social climber who is willing to work to get ahead.

♈ — World leader's spouse. Capable of being legally bound to many people. Morally responsible. Cosmopolitan. Cultured.

☿ — Enamel applied to toenails and fingernails. Nervous wife. Ritual tattoos.

♀ — Male costume jewelry and cosmetics. Mate is lover but not parental. Sweetheart. Attractively proportioned body.

♂ — Limited from participating in normal sports activities.

⚵ — Birth of a male heir. Gynecologist or obstetrician. A licensed midwife.

⚲ — Winner of scholastic honors. Graduated at head of class.

⚳ — Same as above.

⚶ — Barrenness or loss of biological children. Impotent husband or frigid wife.

♃ — Married to fellow convert. Disciplined Christian. Evangelist.

♄ — Devoid of cosmetics or perfume. Facial scars.

⚸ — Signed contract for creative work. Legal papers for publishing novels. Restrictive about public affection.

♆ — Plastic surgery. Hysteria. Hidden neuroses. Nervous collapse.

⚼ — Strictly controlled diet. Extreme self-restraint. Appetite depressant.

⚚ — Member of happy family grouping. Satisfied individual.

⚷ — Not attractive. Body damaged in utero. Congenital nerve deficiencies, causing spastic type reactions.

⚹ — Fertile. Conception of an heir. Mated for breeding.

⚻ — Legally wed. Domineering husband. Specialist. Authoritative.

♃Ⅱ — Married more than once. Well-trained in the classics. Learned restraint.

♇ — Job promotion delayed or thwarted.

☋ — Hidden strengths available when needed.

⚺ — Understands overall purpose of long-term justice. Lives by religious principles.

⚷／☽	Oedipal complex. Jeweled maiden. Final divorce papers. Hour of marriage. Social hostess. Public ceremonies. Female costume jewelry and cosmetics. Feminine wiles.

M — Emotionally uptight.

A — Enjoys formal ceremonies. Wedding attendants. Mother-in-law crying. Expressions of thanks or sympathy.

☉ — Birth of a wanted child. Beloved spouse.

☽ — Same as above.

☊ — Tied to a mother's apron strings. Natural humor and laughter inhibited in large groups.

♈ — The gossip columnist.

☿ — Hypersensitive child. Possible respiratory distress syndrome. Formal invitations.

♀ — Pleasant ceremony. Beautiful and elaborate decorations and certerpieces. Theatrical. Bedecked in finery.

♂ — An alliance of passion.

⚵ — Nurse. Baby-sitter. Companion. Herbal aid to digestive problems.

⚶ — Child of prominent figure. Upheld status of mother. Born into established structure. Wedding consultants. Gift wrap.

⚷ — Same as above.

⚳ — Accept the role of martyr for mate.

♃ — Financially fortunate. Insurance pays for nice funeral. Memorial service. Love a crippled child.

♄ — Loss of ancestral home. Veil of seclusion. Away from the mate. Adopted.

♅ — Civic ceremonies. Breaks ground graciously. Initiates new forms into accepted norm without shocking public.

♆ — Charismatic teacher. Appealed to the upper-class or social leaders. Confused public economic structure.

♇ — Can rouse public emotion and yet remain restrained.

⚴ — Happy marriage of fortunate individuals. Wedding catering. Close ties with the mother.

⚸ — Divorce. Cares for family antiques or records.

⚚ — Fire in old homestead. Forceful mother.

⚼ — To announce the birth of a prince or long-awaited heir. Female mayor or judge.

⚶ — Woman ambassador or delegate. Wife of an important government official. Professor's spouse.

⚥ — Stale marriage. Woman imprisoned by marital responsibility or incarcerated by society.

⚦ — Shy. Keeps away from public gatherings. Enjoys quiet family pleasures.

⚲ — Platonic love. Idealized mother figure. Separated from parents at an early age.

78

⚵ / ☊	Homemaker. Connections with in-laws. Treasury association. Employed by the I.R.S. Connected with traditional people. Linked by propriety. Conservative relatives.

M — Likes being married. Associates with members of established community. Observes rules of etiquette in public.

A — Surrounded by admirers. Wealthy. Born into an outstanding family. Well-bred.

☉ — Day of the wedding. Marital union.

☽ — Public formalization of union. Signing legal papers. Public installation. Mothered by strangers or agency. Mother strict.

☊ — Same as above.

♈ — Financial success after much time and effort.

☿ — Signing of a treaty. Highly published business or alliance. Newsworthy association. News of home. Keeps family journal.

♀ — Cosmetics industry. Luxurious health and diet spa. Grudging compliments.

♂ -- Filled a relative's shoes. Supervised marriage of a brother. Fulfilled a family responsibility.

♁ — Formal public gardens. Limited nursing care.

⚵ — Critical analysis. Report card or evaluation. Strict grade.

⚴ — Same as above.

↓ — Suffers from serious allergies. Allergic reactions checked.

♃ — Wealthy but proper connections.

♄ — Marriage or divorce counselor appointed by the court.

♅ — Changes from childhood teachings or traditions. Appointed to a unique position. Only woman ruler of Rome. Later life.

♆ — Joined a religious order. Mystical union of spirits. Married to convictions. Avowed bride of Christ.

♇ — Upheaval from traditional connections. Protocol changes. Home disrupted by serious illness or war.

⚸ — Fortunate heritage. Good family background. To marry into a happy and well-to-do family.

⊕ — Purify a diseased internal organ. Change legal associations. Wife taken to doctor. Social taboos.

⚶ — Wartime alliance entered into quickly. Quick tongue.

↑ — Association of military school headmasters. Absolute authority.

⚌ — Trains counselors. Study of relationships.

⚚ — Restores the family reputation. Drawn into a scandal by proximity to suspect associates.

△ — Aide to top-notch professionals.

♓ — Formal connection with spiritual people. Baptism or confirmation ceremony. Raised by zealous relatives.

79

City or state celebration. Population control. Marriage laws. Family trends. Dairy trade. Structured world unit. Public ceremonies.

M — Inclined to behave according to strict rules of conduct when attending public gatherings. Rather affectionate in private.

A — Member of a noteworthy family.

☉ — Orthodox wedding ceremony. Married by a recognized priest. An ordination in a major world religion.

☽ — Diplomacy and diplomatic functions. A public ceremony which arouses emotions.

☊ — Associated with those forming public opinion.

♈ — Same as above.

☿ — Travel with spouse who is serviceman. Younger than mate. Wants to "save" others from their own desires. Forceful.

♀ — Wed to his own voice. Contented in rather confined situations. Determined to have one's own way.

♂ — Arrogant. Catalyst. Antagonizes interviewers. The typical male chauvinist.

⚳ — Strictly supervised nursery school or health care center.

⚴ — Renown marriage counselor.

⚵ — Same as above.

⚶ — Bringing tradition to the world, yet eccentric ideas of money.

♃ — Wealthy. Born to riches and fame.

♄ — Lives in a secluded area. Temporary times of isolation.

♅ — Unexpected change of social customs. Breach of etiquette.

♆ — World feels mate was deceitful. Unclear about marital laws. Dreams of loving and famous spouse.

♇ — Disruption in the heart of the city. Realigning of social units. Convulsion caused by birth pains.

⚷ — Famous family name.

⊕ — Study of primitive marriage rites.

⚔ — Military wedding ceremony. Art of fencing.

♈ — National leader. Marital status aired in the news.

♃Ⅱ — Formal banquet complete with appropriate music.

⚵ — Tragedy of life made public. Book about her suffering written to aid others. Kept emotions under control for husband.

⚖ — Draws large crowds.

⚹ — Sanctuary or altar restricted to the public. Commemorate.

80

☿/♀	Demands fairness in all dealings. Formal signing of a bill or document. Tallies everything. Wedding or party invitations. Book about costume jewelry and pyramids.

M — Needs peer and sibling approval for security and satisfaction.

A — Thinks of early marriage. Incorporating small group or club.

⊙ — Underground railroad trips. Careful clipping or cutting of skin or material. Functional small, tight stitches.

☽ — Receives payment for reflections. Public speech. Entertain.

☊ — Multiple alliances and/or legal relationships.

♈ — Public speaking from prepared manuscript.

☿ — Same as above.

♀ — Loved by conservative parents. Difficult about touching and stroking. Nervous but handsome.

♂ — Small-scale procedure works wonders. Laws established. Conference convenes. Social customs reactivated.

⚷ — Formal talk about medical astrology. Purification explained.

⚥ — Well-groomed hands. Tailored. Fine detailing.

☖ — Same as above.

☋ — Husband or wife left home.

♃ — Charming. Appeals to the opposite sex. Married to a younger man or woman.

♄ — Strict guardian or supervisor. Great age difference between partners or mates.

♅ — Unexpected meetings or invitations. Striking blend of colors and fabrics. Mechanics of engineering.

♆ — Misunderstands the role of mother and wife. Escapes from husband and children. Married in name only.

♇ — Mate's chattering disturbs this nervous person.

⚵ — Proper thoughts of love. Typical home life depicted.

⊕ — Communicates by artificial means. Sign language or hearing aid necessary. Needs to understand others.

⚸ — Desires a masterful spouse. Sharp tongued mate.

☊ — Meticulous. Elaborate ceremonies.

♉ — Small circle of very social friends. Not affectionate. Multi-lingual mate.

☿ — Delay in mailing invitations.

△ — Superior intelligence. Structured into useful channels. Potentially explosive mate. Argument brings danger.

⚹ — Delivers inspired and comprehensive sermon. Wrote booklet about occult meanings of pyramid power.

Period of celibacy. Legal inheritance. In love with the idea of matrimony. Love of security. Beauty operator. Hand movements. Entertain as a hostess. Affectionate mate.

M — Artistic and extravagant. Enjoys formal gatherings.

A — Birth of a girl child. Socially prominent parents.

☉ — Putting one in a position of danger. Harmful nervous tension. Negligence. Beauty operator.

☽ — Emotional satisfaction and happiness in marriage. Shows off lovely jewelry for visitors. Pride in possessions.

♌ — Around socially conscious people. Expected to attend formal gatherings. Snobbish.

♈ — Public acclaim for tasks well-done. Newsworthy. Married for prestige.

☿ — Enchanting. Joyful chatter. Cheerful thoughts.

♀ — Same as above.

♂ — Forlorn. Working closely with groups. = Saturn, son of company president.

♀ — Bachelor or spinster who enjoys being around family and children or friends. Good physical build.

♀ — Brief disruption in marital bliss.

⚴ — Same as above.

↓ — Birth of a girl. Cosmetic mesh. Dedication ceremony.

♃ — Large formal party. Mate overindulges. Protects golden artifacts. Entertainments flourish.

♄ — Unwanted birth of girl child. Beautician by profession. Father's heritage involved.

♓ — Pregnancy with a girl child. Change-of-life baby. Change of direction.

♆ — Understands the colors and structures of auras. Social deception. Unmailed or mislaid invitation.

♇ — Love affair.

⚵ — Attractively dressed. Good clothes sense. Addition to the family.

⊕ — Abuse of wife or child. Magnetic anthropologist. Death of love or lover.

⚶ — A woman's fertility. Fertility rites.

⚷ — Financial counselor. Anointed with oils.

⚸ — Female scholar. Trained for work with women's problems.

⚹ — Restricted appetites and desires. Lonely hours of woman.

⚺ — Subtle pressures and powers.

⚻ — Dedicated a life to the ministry. "Called" to a higher purpose. To consecrate the life's work.

Irritable, working spouse. Structured emotions and drive. Cesarean section. Rebellious man. Structuring and containing anger. Married man.

M — Overly aggressive around active men.

A — Spouse irritated by associates. Volatile temper.

☉ — Armed with fortitude of convictions. Evangelistic zeal. Military reforms.

☽ — Drove wife to work. Kissed mate goodbye. Absolute devotion. Left for job-related travel.

☊ — Knows an agitated man. Wall Street lawyer or broker. Important connections.

♈ — Marital strife becomes public knowledge. Critical of partner. Wardrobe mistress for large theatrical company.

☿ — Verbal attack on traditions or customs.

♀ — Inherited a gift of pearls. Preached against unnecessary luxuries. Impatient when denied presents. Music soothes.

♂ — Same as above.

? — Mother is strict disciplinarian. Angry working wife. Chain, to legal contract chafes.

⚷ — Seamstress. New job contract offered and accepted. Marriage of competent actor and actress. Wed to equal.

⚸ — Same as above.

☋ — Separation from legal spouse. Transferred away from family and loved ones.

♃ — Overextended. Too many gentlemen and too few workers. Tempers flare. Energy for sports rather than work.

♄ — Relationship with older married man. Father figure strong.

♅ — Divorce, Nervous breakdown. Battered his wife. Nervous tension. Unusual sexual activities.

♆ — Searching for a soulmate. Idealistic concept of marriage.

♇ — Breakup of marriage, or partnership.

⚴ — Professional involvements take place of family concerns.

⚵ — Challenging old beliefs and standard practices.

⚶ — Vindictiveness. Controls reactions.

⚷ — Dislikes authority or being bossed.

⚳ — Persistent professor. Tenacious about proving discoveries.

⚹ — Traditional funeral. Discreet sex life. Periods of decreased energy. Fulfilling social duties.

⚺ — Married to a very influential person in their common business or company.

⚻ — Criticizes moral behavior. Inspired distractions.

83

Duty before satisfaction. Handicapped spouse. Raped. Partners dedicated to same goal or religious ideals. Sexually incapacitated or damaged. Remains unwed.

M — Remains dignified in an embarassing situation.

A — Married for political or business reasons. Lack of affection.

☉ — Stands firm concerning family traditions. Physical release demanded. Blood ties.

☽ — Death of maternal relative. Care of crippled child. Female problems with hardening of uterus. Illness of mother.

☊ — Trapped by a marriage.

♈ — Tremendous world changes. Realignment of boundaries, allies.

☿ — Loss of child. Thoughts of marriage breakup. Assaulted by close friend. Careful of expressions. Frustrated.

♀ — Financial gain from sale of jewelry. Flaunts sensuality or hides it completely.

♂ — Restrained from sexual fulfillment with husband or wife.

⚳ — Care of stepdaughters increased. Foster child assaulted. Loss of a child.

⚢ — Accepted public speaking engagement. Strictly disciplined. Enforces the law.

⚥ — Same as above.

⚥ — Same as above.

♃ — Couple found help for handicapped child.Love out of wedlock.

♄ — Remains unmarried to care for aging parent. Sexual perverversion. Harmful assault and rape. Body damaged.

♅ — Change current social or moral standards. Discreet commitment to reform.

♆ — Brief marriage to film matinee idol. Remaining immature. Not yet ripe.

♇ — Disruptive rituals or ceremonies. Sudden grief. Protest.

⚴ — Nun. Priest or minister in the family.

⚘ — Giving polarity treatment. Adjusting and realigning.

⚷ — Installed as commander of armed forces.

♈ — Married by the clergyman. Crowned ruler of country. Accept legal responsibility in impressive ceremony.

♃ — Invented out of necessity.

⚕ — Lived in seclusion. Family extremely protective. Chronic congenital defect.

⚹ — Nervous strain.

⚻ — Murdered for humanitarian reasons. Innocently caught up in a worldwide crisis. Deeply sympathetic.

Wealthy and pleasing mate. Well-educated husband or wife. True helpmate. Spouse won over lover. Overfeeding. Wife assisting husband's growth. Successful cosmotologist.

M — Public celebration of achievements. Uptight and nervous.

A — Extravagant people. Luxurious tour group.

☉ — Wealthy and prosperous. Sense of propriety. Peer approval. Proper host. Overtaxing body.

☽ — Public honors. Sensual and happy couple. Reacts emotionally to subjective events.

♌ — Rich but proper connections. Prim ties.

♈ — Priest. Rabbi. Minister. Professor of religious traditions and history. Well-known.

☿ — Marriage to a writer. Husband handles research and schedules for his mate and partner.

♀ — Surrounded by stately gardens and furnishings. Born to the gentry. Socially acceptable.

♂ — Fluctuating finances create tension between mates. Spendthrift. Live hand-to-mouth.

? — Pilot broke the rules.

♀ — Successful novelist. Writes understandably about love and marriage.

⚇ — Same as above.

↓ — Abolitionist. Sacrifice much for career and family. Loss of titles and land. Eliminates buttons and ornaments.

♃ — Same as above.

♄ — Separated from mate. Divorce. Critical of spouse. Shadows on a happy marriage. Decrease of joint funds.

♅ — Innovative yet remaining traditional in format.

♆ — Confusion in marriage. Bled to death. A dreamer.

♇ — Restricted activities and funds. Unable to fully enjoy exalted position in life. Brutal rage.

⚷ — The enlarged family gathering or reunion.

⚳ — Widowed. Varicose veins. Health problems from obesity.

⚵ — Addition to household. Expansion or remodeling of home.

♈ — Female executive. Financial status potentially expansive. Good legal advice. Marries a tall man.

⚴ — Appreciated. Properly congratulated or acknowledged. An approved alliance.

⚶ — Shared renovation or restoration of old homestead.

⚸ — Unusual success or popularity.

⚹ — The high priest or priestess.

⚹/♄	Fulfilled responsibilities to mate. Burdened by having an incapacitated spouse. Clouds over a marriage. Prudish. Partner ill or recuperating.

M — Feeling tied down by excessive responsibilities. A definite need for stability in relationships.

A — Divorce, separation from mate. Leaving family. Being away from family celebrations and customs.

⊙ — Going through a long period of evaluation to find self. = Pluto Shouldered responsibility for mate's changes.

☽ — Guardian of widow's funds. Surrounded by women. Chauvinistic. Strong and vocal supporter of women's rights.

☊ — Because of cold marriage, mate found solace in groups.

♈ — Announced separation. Embarassing situation obvious to all.

☿ — Overly rigid childhood training. Disciplined harshly. Embarassed at displays of affection.

♀ — Small, regular shaped teeth. Large boned woman. Depleted metabolism. Calcium absorption inhibited.

♂ — Resents men silencing women. To choose an abusive husband. Added to spouse's pressures. A bore. Irritated illness.

? — Shunned accepted burdens of citizenship. Lack of social or popular acceptance. Product of a broken home.

⚢ — Worked alongside older and more accomplished partner.

⚸ — Same as above.

↓ — Cared for sick wife. Melancholy. Shouldered emotional burdens. Accepted criticism of convictions.

♃ — Dependable mate supports handsomely. Friendly yet aloof even with family members. Determined.

♄ — Same as above.

♓ — Sudden changes in marital state. Abrasions on the skin.

♆ — Resents misunderstandings. Alcoholic mate depresses. Idealistic about marriage. Reacts irrationally when molded.

♇ — Breakup of partners. Betrothal dissolved. Ugly divorce. Impotent. Domestic upheaval.

⚩ — Attractive or handsome mate. Embarassed by associated. Age span for marriage partners.

⊕ — Financial difficulties cloud marriage prospects.

⚷ — Forced separation from family. Delay of commitment.

♈ — Bossy. Dictatorial. Accustomed to speaking imperatively.

⚷ — Stresses the older, more conservative theories and approach in scientific research.

⚵ — Overcoming tight finances. End of difficult relationship.

⚴ — Working against strong odds.

⚳ — Dreamed of becoming famous. Worshipped successful political figures. Deified gold.

| | Elopement. Sudden breakup of family. Unorthodox ceremonies. Multiple marriages. Eruptions in relationships. Complex and unusual communities or units. |

M — Unorthodox thoughts and views of marriage.

A — Prone to grand entrances at inopportune moments. Warped.

☉ — Wants to get married suddenly.

☽ — Odd birth circumstances. Married to unusual woman. Faced with demands of a changing role. Sex clarification.

♌ — Shouldered responsibility for which not trained.

♈ — Remembered as a lovely paramour.

☿ — Unexpected news of wedding. Quick marriage of necessity. Multiple identities. Numerous name changes.

♀ — Brides arrived by the shipload. Multiple marriages brought happiness. Unusual family structure worked well.

♂ — Sudden wedding of male relative.

♩ — Naturally disruptive. Volcanic.

⚳ — Task of breaking down cultural barriers. Translate remnants of a civilization into contemporary terms.

⚴ — Same as above.

↓ — To verbalize social protests.

♃ — Successful change of habits. Irregular romantic arrangement. Ballooning of constricted artery.

♄ — Suddenly accused. Reforms denied on questioned construction.

♓ — Same as above.

♆ — Confusion causes erratic changes in life pattern and habits. Uncertain about sense of values.

♀ — Diplomat.

♃ — Eventful marriage. Husband and wife who maintain good relationship despite separations. Peaceful leave-taking.

⊕ — Abuse of child. Unexpected intestinal illness of wife.

⚹ — Sudden romance with powerful man. Forceful political dignitary honored for heroic action.

♈ — Elopement of father. Intervention through highest channels of government.

♃Ⅱ — Professional scientific community.

♀ — Spewing forth filth and disease. Harsh, angry words.

⚸ — Explosive breakup of marriage or partnership.

♓ — Unorthodox religious ceremonies. Communion of rebels. Spiritualist groups inspired by unusual methods.

87

⚵/♆	Confusion in a marriage. Alcoholic mate. Dissolution of a legal tie. Secret problems threatening one's purse. Unexpected sexual advance. Sending rumors of recession.

M — Dreams of elevated social position. Unrealistic basis for idea.

A — Unstable family life. Born while parents are overseas from their homeland.

☉ — Dream of marriage. Disillusioned by mate. = Mercury, hearing damage resulting from medication taken by mother.

☽ — Confusion. Fraud. Embezzlement. Double-dealing. Dreamer. Visionary.

☊ — Bigamist unveiled.

♈ — Appears virginal. Trusting innocence.

☿ — Lies about upholding traditions. Uses pen names. Chaired an importance religious conference. Debate theological issues.

♀ — Enjoys painting landscapes and ocean scenes. Absent-minded hostess.

♂ — Working to make daydreams come true. Irritable. Emotionally disturbed. Employed in a winery.

⚳ — Loses children to former spouse in legal settlement. Born of missionary parents.

⚴ — Sculpts in clay as a hobby. Researches historical periods and genealogical documents in career.

⚵ — Same as above.

⚶ — Died peacefully. Bladder infection of female.

♃ — Skillful use of cosmetics to conceal medical problem. Good at covering-up confusion. Travel. Masking.

♄ — Integrity questioned by authorities. Partner convicted of fraud. Closely connected by scandals.

♅ — Gawky kid. Allows self to be brunt of jokes. Develops a caricature. Sudden disillusionment about spouse.

♆ — Same as above.

♇ — Regenerate through illusion of marriage. Repeated sexual affair. Unfaithful. Sex change. Evolving moral standards.

⯠ — Desire marriage to soulmate. Dissolve outgrown family ties. Love undermined by fear of loss. Emotional panic.

⯡ — Broken engagement. Romantic dreams not fulfilled.

⯢ — Not fertile. Alcoholic rehabilitation. Near miscarriage.

⯣ — Well-known romance novelist.

⯥ — Plays in local symphony orchestra. Trained musician.

⯦ — Necessary documents destroyed by flood.

⯧ — Healing salves for burns.

⯤ — Sings in church choir. Delivers impressive prayer.

<table>
<tr><td>⚇/♀</td><td>Bossy and jealous spouse. Real letdown. Upheaval of social morals. Intense marital desire. Breaking of the marriage vows. Bereavement. Social activist.</td></tr>
</table>

M — Discontented with position in life. Alarmist.

A — Divided family interests.

☉ — Frustrated male. Estranged from husband.

☽ — Transformation of woman's marriage. Weeping widow.

☊ — Social climber. Olfactory sensitivity makes it difficult to be in crowds. Campaign against moral corruption.

♈ — Publicly reprimanded. Fired for unorthodox behavior. Reports of a scandalous romance.

☿ — Social protester. Uses traditional methods to teach about occult materials.

♀ — Released wife or female partner. Industrial accident left several widows. Friends supported for a time.

♂ — Discovered the insights of working together on specific projects. Liberal male supporter.

? — Disappointed by feud between children.

♀ — Entering a brand new career endeavor. Transformed from an apprentice into a professional.

⚳ — Same as above.

↓ — Preached to those in prison. Sudden loss of child. Led spiritual revivals. Tragic loss of family member.

♃ — Buried alive.

♄ — Personal relationship changed into business agreement. Lover now employee. Escape from battering husband.

♅ — Symbols of changing social order. Reversed the normal masculine, feminine roles in a relationship.

♆ — Imagined that men wanted to rape her. Broken down or dissolved social code of the day.

♇ — Same as above.

⚴ — Legal maneuver to protect an invention.

⚵ — Rotten eggs. Fertilizer for flower garden or shrub border. Headaches caused by allergies.

⚶ — Shot mate. Argumentative and destructive partnership. Great upheavals.

♈ — Tall. Attracts attention because of commanding appearance. Pituitary malfunction.

⚷ — Eventually rises above problems. Achieves despite handicap.

⚸ — Patiently waits for suitable timing. Develops precise darkroom techniques for photographic practice.

⚺ — Drastic change of lifestyle. Powerful incentive to influence morals of the community.

♓ — Institutionalized for psychoanalysis.

Happy marriage rite or ceremony. Beloved partner. Host or hostess for family celebrations or holidays. Artistic spouse who becomes famous. Observes proper conduct in relations.

M — Supportive of partner's drive for higher office.

A — Interrelated projects. Marriage between cousins.

⊙ — Small but close family unit. Studious relatives.

☽ — Gracious hostess. Enjoys family. Lives near relatives.

☊ — Born of a love match. Close ties. Adored by relatives.

♈ — Social dinner or dance.

☿ — Sister-in-law of several radicals.

♀ — Famous romance writer. Successful combination.

♂ — Office in the home.

♃ — Overly concerned mother. Cares for lost animals, adopts pets.

⚵ — Fits and sells wedding gowns. Creates floral arrangements for weddings, funerals, etc. Uses flowers for healing.

⚴ — Same as above.

⚳ — Demands control of family partnership finances.

♃ — Successful partnerships. Content among approving followers. Celibate. Good fortune. Large, close-knit family.

♄ — Ending of happy marriage. Loss of beloved husband or wife through illness or senility.

♅ — Erratic about funds. Importance of budgeting money and time.

♆ — Unrealistic legal structure. Deceived by relations or mate. Group gives illusion of harmony. Cult.

♇ — Marriage ends in disaster. Disruptive union.

⚷ — Same as above.

⚸ — Primitive vacation cabin. Simple temporary living style.

⚚ — Compatible sexual responses. Fertility.

⚶ — Legally handles the family funds.

⚼ — Exhibits the power of positive thinking.

⚹ — Loss of beloved mate.

⚲ — Fulfilling a long-cherished desire.

⚻ — Spiritual ties. Church congregation. True humility.

| ⚷/⊕ | Need for marital counseling. Attitude unpopular with social peers. Killing the institution of marriage. Disastrous love life. Imprisoned. |

M — Served in prison social work and reform.

A — Disgusted by relatives by marriage.

⊙ — Chronic illness in later years. Inhibiting physical condition.

☽ — Veils intense feelings in public. Emotionally devastated.

☋ — Grief seen by many curiosity seekers. Taken to morgue by associates. Connected by tragedy.

♈ — Openly showing disapproval. Hopsacking or other rough material. Downfall or firing of a vice president.

☿ — Decorating magazine featuring antiques. Funeral litany. Severe headache.

♀ — Cautious about displaying affection. Restrained person. Mudpack facial. Tarnished jewels.

♂ — Building up a compost heap. Preparing the flower beds for planting.

? — Amiable and agreeable in most instances.

⚲ — Denial or delay of marriage because of job commitments.

⚷ — Same as above.

↓ — Impoverished widow. A vindictive woman. Clinging vine which kills its support. A parasite.

♃ — Scolded for using cosmetics. Advantages of orthodox behavior. Strict parental training. Conservative religions.

♄ — Physical care of aged parents. Encumbered by serious duties. Liable for another.

♓ — Arrested. Scocking scandal. Disruptive.

♆ — Lovers quarrel. Unreliable mate. Superstitious. Protocol error.

♇ — Determined to succeed. Needs to achieve.

♃ — Financial problems for a corporate structure. Family struggle. Group of archeologists facing a difficult dig.

⊕ — Same as above.

⚸ — Violent marital arguments. Destruction of marriage.

↑ — Official biography. Leader in aid for battered children and wives. Spearheaded projects to aid population problems.

♃Ⅱ — Friendship with married persons. Corrupt business deals.

⚵ — Aversion to marriage.

⚼ — The shamed wife. Self-consciousness. Compulsive collector of junk.

♓ — Exposed to some bitter concepts of marriage and fidelity. Giving allegiance to religious discipline instead of mate.

91

⚥ / ↕ ↕	Sharp knife or sword. Scapel. Anticipated remarriage. Strong and authoritative female. Strict disciplinarian. Rational mind.

M — Mother or mother-in-law of a large family. Respects all strong authority figures.

A — Raised by a strict mother. From a military background. The DAR member. Influences many people.

☉ — Destined for important roles. Self-esteem. Forceful.

☽ — Perceptive about superior. Intuitive, but secretive.

☋ — Married to a person with influential connections.

♈ — Patent of a new procedure.

☿ — Outspokenness upsets temperamental spouse. Sharp tongue.

♀ — Overweight. Glandular deficiency.

♂ — Surgery. Clean, clinical delivery.

♀ — Leader among women of her time. Civic leader.

♀ — Tailor or seamstress. Comprehensible writer. Appreciates the importance of detailed research.

⚥ — Same as above.

↓ — Can cut away superfluous debris to care for matters. Calm under fire or in a crisis. Ritual circumcision.

♃ — Cautious about accepting benefits of fame and fortune.

♄ — Trimming away all surplus skin or material. Pruning. A very strict diet. Basic humility.

♆ — Driven by ambition. Twenty-one gun salute. Sharply rebuked for social slight.

♅ — Naive. Foolishly expected great returns.

♇ — Move. Upset social patterns.

⚵ — Planned parenthood. Military wedding ceremony. Celebration cut short by violence.

⊕ — Improperly formed. Genetic mutations.

⚸ — Same as above.

♈ — Active in local politics. Strict belief in party policies. Headed fund-raising drive for mission maternity clinic.

♃ — Trained marriage counselor.

⚤ — Mechanical fastener. Durable qualities. Devices to provide compressed air.

⚠ — Helpless to prevent stabbing. Heedless of accepted procedures. Break record. Strongly motivated to mutilate self.

⚹ — Not really open to new ideas. Questioning the intuition. Investigation of religious ideals.

| ⚛ / ♈ | Priest or rabbi handling ritual matters. Head of the social register. Accepted by the "in" group. Married to a public figure. |

M — Gracious acceptance of honors. Self-confident. Good lineage.

A — Public acclaim given by head of department. Congratulations.

☉ — The dignified host. Able to discriminate.

☽ — The poised woman. Statuesque. Discreet.

☊ — Born into a leading family. Royal heir. Binds firmly together. Securely attached or closed.

♈ — Informative news release. Distantly related to nobility. Wife temporarily in command. Gains through marriage.

☿ — Adapts methods of showing affection to suit his or her purpse. Quick wits behind a cold facade.

♀ — Wife succeeds husband in high government office. Power of a pleasing personality. Gained support by being congenial.

♂ — Married by priest or bishop. Argument with pastor.

? — Physical and emotional distance between parent and child.

♀ — Received a scholarship because of family circumstances.

⚛ — Same as above.

↓ — Plead to captor for mercy. Sexual initiation. Memorable introduction of maiden.

♃ — Successful mate. Allied with a handsome and prominent man or beautiful and prosperous woman.

♄ — Denial of promotion. Loss of deceased husband's bonus.

♓ — Unexpected good fortune creates turning point in lifestyle.

♆ — Great deception concerning equality.

♇ — Exchanged duties between business partners. Review of the relationship.

⚷ — Daughter of the governor or leader. Devout missionary family. Leaders in a small community.

⊕ — Humiliated by reprimand from superior.

⚸ — Forceful assertion of self.

♈ — Same as above.

⚵ — Well trained by a professional in the area of expertise. Accepted into an exclusive fraternity or circle.

⚶ — Patient with rules and regulations. Good family heritage. Defeated by brute strength. Killed during drunken revelry.

⚹ — Torn from relationship with influential person.

⚺ — Inspired preacher or lecturer. Leading theological scholar.

M —	Achiever. Top of the class. Excellent education.
A —	Reliable relatives. Professor's daughter or wife. Classmates at graduation ceremony.
☉ —	Fame and money received.
☽ —	Simple but lovable woman. Healing hands and voice. Comforts others.
☊ —	Among trained educators. Fraternizes with the elite. Finds friends among a chosen few. Selective about associates.
♈ —	Fortunate. Good public relations. Bested the previous record.
☿ —	Best-selling romance writer. Careful sentence construction. Bilingual.
♀ —	Paired with fashion expert. Sultry singer. Successful popular musician. Lyric writer. Brillant mind confined.
♂ —	Married to an engineer. Husband becomes able manager.
? —	A natural teacher. Intuitive understanding of what pupils comprehend or where there is confusion.
⚥ —	Member of MENSA.
⚴ —	Same as above.
⚷ —	Recuperates away from family. Active churchwoman.
♃ —	Receiving a diploma or college degree.
♄ —	Spouse received advanced degree. Husband graduated.
⚸ —	Eccentric wife. Raises quantities of wild flowers. Good, but untrained vocal qualities.
♆ —	Famous romance author. Dreams of an alliance with the social elite.
♇ —	Location of prestigious gatherings. Aging landmark. Complete renovation. Face-lift.
⚴♀ —	An understanding and educated mate brings joy. Wed philosopher.
⊊ —	Research the past. Counsels students with fear of failure.
⚵ —	Projected into a wider social scene. Circulating among the aristocracy. Associated with cultural elite.
♈ —	Well-known author of romance novels. Public relations director for nudist colony.
♃Ⅱ —	Same as above.
♀̶ —	Death ends family celebration and traditions. Lack of an education or scholastic degree causes some embarassment.
⚶ —	Propelled into high legal office. Woman lawyer.
⚹ —	Worship in traditional church. Helpmate. Marriage partner of like ideal and spirit. Fellow sufferer. Destined companion.

⚵ / ⚷	Control of reproduction. Loss of mate. Terminate the past. Unpleasant marital relationships. Lack of warmth. Pattern for rebirth.

M — Afraid of getting married. Prefers to work alone.

A — Scandals aired under severe stress or suppression of emotions. Influenced by a mentally disturbed friend.

☉ — Defeated by overwhelming odds. End of a long physical struggle. Resting peacefully after difficult exertion.

☽ — Emotional trauma of divorce.

☊ — Field of close acquaintance narrowed by demands of spouse.

♈ — Sale of house papers signed. Openly proud of his or her home no matter how humble it is.

☿ — In process of rehabiliting. Ability to concentrate amid clutter. Discusses doctrines of reincarnation. Annoyed by chatter.

♀ — Jealous. Among females.

♂ — Stable and loyal person. Slow and methodical working habits.

♃ — Primitive sanitary facilities.

⚨ — Suppressing aggression or masculine traits. Fights against male leadership of the time period.

⚹ — Same as above.

☋ — Eliminates everything but the purpose at hand. Exclusive. Builds on past experiences.

♃ — Family secrets. Homestead. Judgmental woman. Widow.

♄ — Established legal precedents in domestic trial.

♆ — An excitable woman. Sudden breakup of long relationship.

♅ — Perversions.

♇ — Face a complete revision of marital relationship.

⚴ — Marriage postponed. Limited career of mate. Deserted by relatives. Death of a parent or in-law.

⚳ — Inherited old house from spouse. Moral corruption. A venereal disease.

⚵ — Fatal injury from firearms. War casualty.

⚶ — Committee for planned parenthood. Administrator of funds for population control. Spearheaded an organization.

⚷ — Loss of early opportunities taught patience. Trained to use rapid responses. Utilizes Oriental movement principles.

⚚ — Same as above.

⚸ — Forced to be realistic.

⚹ — Becoming part of a spiritual community. Period of meditation following spiritual feasting.

⚷ / ☋	Advantageous move. Married to a higher force. Explosion of suppressed emotions. Forced into a wedding ceremony. Influenced by partner.

M — Enjoys power and prestige. Shares husband's glory.

A — Empowered by authority of another.

☉ — Brings groups of important persons to large gatherings. Attractive in a flamboyant way. Opulence.

☽ — Woman who is attuned to higher planes.

☋ — Won the high-jumping prize.

♈ — Regal appearance. Circumspect.

☿ — Unique rephrasing. Quotes authority. Restricted communication.

♀ — A sensual wife. Strong need for security of stable marriage.

♂ — Yearning for success. Able to team with another for combined strengths. Great determination.

⚳ — Forced into marriage because of pregnancy. Cared for by powerful spouse. Dominated by partner.

⚴ — Commissioned to write approved manuscript. Contents restricted by those in charge.

⚵ — Same as above.

⚶ — Wedding delayed by circumstances.

♃ — Empowered to function. Mechanical fastener. Disillusion with parental religion caused loss of spiritual faith.

♄ — Works without the usual assistance. Forced to relearn a way of locking, sealing and protecting.

♅ — Influential. Choice location lost its advantages due to center city change.

♆ — Uplifted by spiritual strength.

♇ — Strong will. Determined not to be defeated by circumstances. Ambitious mate.

♃♀ — Born in a time of social change. Uprooted from family and home. Forced to emigrate to foreign land.

⊕ — Rehabilitation training. Debris remaining from explosion or bombing. Takes in homeless and abandoned.

⚸ — Discipline taught by forceful events.

⚷ — Ceremonies of politics. Political protocol. Forced into a mold as mate of government official.

♃Ⅱ — A true statesman. International concerns. Philanthropist. Universal understanding.

⊕ — Same as above.

☋ — Forced into a corner by pressures of society and family.

⚹ — Intuitive husband or wife.

96

Received costume jewelry. Structured religious organization. Linked by similar dreams and ideals. Reacted too rapidly in legalizing idea and was deceived.

M — Loyal to marriage vows. Accept the spouse's convictions.

A — Gradually drifts away from home and family.

☉ — Romantic. Idealist. Married to charter pilot. Representing a particular segment of church community. Act from conviction.

☽ — Restored to former beauty. Born into a sincere and religious family. Controls sensitivity. Handles relations with finesse.

☊ — Belonged to occult groups. Psychic attunement.

♈ — Priest. Rabbi. Religious scholar specializes in old litany.

☿ — Talks about ideal spouse. Versatile partner.

♀ — Spiritual healer. Beautiful voice, raised in praise to God in religious services.

♂ — Diligent supporter of ordained spouse. Woman who works hard in husband's church.

♃ — Born in Russia. Unbreakable ties to the land. Emotions held in check under sophisticate veneer.

♌ — Subservient and meek outer appearance. Inner core of strength. Ordained minister. Sings hymns.

♓ — Same as above.

↓ — Unusual source of inspiration.

♃ — Conservative religious background.

♄ — Loyal in face of opposition. Accepted marriage as a sacrament. Criticized for putting ideals into action.

♅ — Shaken up by having to face impossibility of dreams being real. Vulnerable to pain of others. Revival. Occasional shocks.

♆ — Prophetic dreams. Wrote nostalgically of other time periods.

♇ — Commitment coming from time of upheaval. Evangelical zest.

♃ — Union of soulmates. Family oriented church. Vows of priest.

⊕ — Shattered dreams or visions of grandeur.

☥ — Zealous priest. Married to cause or career.

♈ — Legal ramifications of priestly commitments and vows.

♃⚏ — Being initiated into a religious order. Ordination of priest. Spiritual union.

⚳ — Delve deeply into customs of the past. Questions orthodox structures. Channels mystic experiences.

⚴ — Inner fortitude in face of severe mistreatment. Events of the parapsychology category.

♓ — Same as above.

M — Goals which are derived from inner beliefs. Personal sacrifices. Rituals which have many meanings. Private altar in home or office. Ability to serve. Personal rituals or rites. Driven by desire for fame and fortune.

M — Same as above.

A — Civic responsibilities take precedence over personal concerns.

☉ — Special type of funeral service. Scaldal. Sacrifice reputation for individual beliefs.

☽ — Reaction to worship service. Personal meditation period. Psychological influence on public.

☊ — To change houses. Frequently move and leave associates in the former location.

♈ — Motivated by religious ideals.

☿ — Denial of personal wishes for study or travel. One who reads the lines on a palm. No girls on the trip.

♀ — Structured responses to romantic advances. Reserved in social situations. Reticent with opposite sex.

♂ — Continues working after reasonable effort has been expended. Futile efforts. Drives self mercilessly.

? — An overly concerned mother or grandparent. Teaches children their early and simple prayers.

⚲ — Suited for a religious vocation. Sunday School teacher.

⚵ — Nervous disposition. Demands obedience from all inferiors. Expects same complete commitment from associates as from self.

↓ — Same as above.

♃ — Blissful. Appreciation of a mass or musical concert.

♄ — Additional responsibilities accepted. Feeling burdened.

♆ — Shattering of one's security basis.

♅ — Idealist. = Sun, Female priest.

♀ — Perseverence. Analytical. Normally careful and cautious.

⚴ — Family chapel. Combined strengths promote chosen issue.

⚷ — Persistent adherence to principles alienated associates.

⚸ — Zealous determination about chosen projects or ideals. Frigid because of early molestation.

♈ — Wants to chair charitable fund-raising drive. Accepts the principles of paternalism comfortably.

⚶ — The educated clergyman. Working in a seminary or convent. Very strict Mother Superior.

⚵ — Very persistent. Measure of spiritual training on psychic powers brings about physical and emotional inbalance.

⚶ — Divinely guided. Receives directions from invisible sources.

⚹ — Enlightened disciple of major ashram. Awakening to soul's true pathway. Opening of chakras.

98

| | Location of a sacred shrine. Lodge or temple of secret organization. Charitable institutions. Periods of isolation. Uncompromising. Dreams of special goals. Noncompetitive. Inner joy unseen by world. Cannot explain ideals. |

M — Keeper of the special shrine. Not ambitious in a material way. Penetrating gaze. The doorkeeper.

A — Same as above.

☉ — Looks to charismic male image for security. Willing servant.

☽ — Putting aside individual life to care for needy mother. Responding to maternal instincts.

☊ — Surrounded by obligations. Set aside family for principles.

♈ — Noteworthy or notorious relative.

☿ — Tied down by details.

♀ — Seen by others as a perpetual virgin. Inhibited during casual contacts. Has difficulty showing affection.

♂ — Shrine dedicated to military personnel. = Neptune, Unknown soldier. Angry body. Frustrated. Jealous.

♁ — An uncompromising nursemaid or baby sitter.

♀ — Uses business acumen in aiding charity funds. Proselytes.

♇ — The obstinate mate. A critical and frustrated wife.

↓ — Same as above.

♃ — Breaks with crowd over religious issues.

♄ — Involved in serious traffic accident. Psychological changes due to near fatal situation.

♓ — The clown shows through the tears.

♆ — Follower of a deluded cleric. Easily swayed by emotional persuasion. A recent convert. Brainwashed by priest.

♀ — Trying to decide what to give up in life. Martyrdom.

♃♀ — Denying family and social life for other desires.

⊕ — A person who gets to the bottom of things. Isolation from surroundings for a set purpose.

⚧ — Possible sexual perversion in intimate relationships. Strongly suppresses ego for pledged duties. Loyal.

⚷ — Legally assuming responsibility for a relative. Getting power of attorney or curatorship. Admired organizer.

♃Ⅱ — Church-related college or boarding school. Strict professor.

⚹ — Firm convictions and classical understanding of lecturer.

⚴ — Single-minded convert.

⚸ — Offered spiritual comfort to diseased and dying.

↓/⊙	Serious but calm personality. Day of a dedication ceremony. Main or central altar in a sanctuary. Well-preserved body. Bound by an unfortunate alliance. Changes in life's direction.

M — Time of consecration service. Karmic responsibilities. Firm convictions realized and accepted.

A — Beloved. Appreciated. Others feel the concern.

⊙ — Same as above.

☽ — Body crippled by polio halted dance career. Sadness.

☊ — Denial of power or recognition from associates.

♈ — World Day of Prayer. Reputed as unusual or eccentric person.

☿ — Spokesperson for others. Unselfish. Bronchial illness.

♀ — Hysterectomy. Cheerful, but sober commitment.

♂ — Men subvert the native's right to authority.

♀ — Pleasant appearance. Country setting.

♀ — Works as a nun. Day of priest's ordination.

♃ — Sanctified priest. Keeps distance between self and others.

↓ — Same as above.

♃ — Overtaxed the heart. Carried many burdens out of sense of dedication. Committed man.

♄ — Depressed by worry and concern for husband or father.

♓ — Sudden divorce. Commitment to old order. Eccentric old priest.

♆ — Uncertain health conditions.

♀ — Purged of sense of mission. Consistently loses children into custody of other parent. Eruptions.

♃ — Forced to shoulder marital responsibilities. Conservative religious background. Raised by "pillars of the community."

♁ — Placed in precarious position. Face life or death issue.

⚵ — Burned to death in explosion. Separated by war or gunfire.

♈ — On welfare or receiving government aid.

♃ — Express appreciation for retiring teacher's faithful service.

♀ — Placed in protective custody. Impeachment threatened.

⚴ — Endless energies sent in pursuit of interests.

⚳ — Spiritual service. Male virgin. Monk or lama. Lay self at the altar of sacrifice.

100

↓/ ⟩	Closing the solar plexis chakra. Public dedication. **Martyr** complex. Mothering self by drinking quantities of milk or dairy products. Sacrifice of emotions. Public altars.

M — Keeps sexual preferences private or secret. Side altars.

A — Worships a dead friend. Believes in communication with ancestors and dead. Friends with a religious eccentric.

⊙ — Feeling unloved and misunderstood because of defense of personal beliefs. Weak body but strong spirit.

☽ — Same as above.

☊ — Ministers to groups of deprived women. Licensed female preacher. Public ordination.

♈ — Forgotten by world or refuted by current hypothesis.

☿ — Undertaking large-scale responsibilities. Serious student.

♀ — Sacrifice motherhood willingly. Emotional trauma causes kidney damage. Perpetual virgin. Suppress personal desires.

♂ — Tireless under pressure. Expends limitless energies serving the public. Working for a cause.

? — Adopts a retarded child.

⚲ — Public servant. Evening hours devoted to work.

⚴ — Ordained minister. Final vows of nun. Barren matron.

↓ — Same as above.

♃ — Woman who accepts religious vocation. Cries at funerals.

♄ — Public disgrace for political stand. Discerning historian.

♅ — Unexpected emotional disruptions. Changes religious rites. Rebel against outside interference with personal beliefs.

♆ — Forlorn. One whom time passes by unnoticed.

♇ — Makes drastic changes in lifestyle after conversion. A demanding personality. Hidden love of danger.

♃ — Married to a religious fanatic. Family who takes vows of poverty because of shared beliefs. Distressed partners.

⊕ — History buff. Disregarding ethical principles.

⇑ — Crusader. Killed for a cause. Becomes the pawn in a struggle between two ideologies.

↑ — Rebels against foster mother's rules.

♃Ⅱ — Refuses to adapt to community standards. Functioning out of guilt complex. Unusual mother-child relationship.

⚵ — Strong self-control. Emotional discipline.

⚳ — Dire need to avoid anxiety and melancholy.

⚻ — Missionary. Nun. Female virgin. Need for self-control and emotional discipline. Spiritual dedication.

101

M — Looks forward to devoting energies to a specific cause.

A — Loyal member of an exclusive group. Small, but close, family. Members of a minority sect.

⊙ — Connected with a religious community of believers. Church related. Blood kin to a priest or minister.

☽ — Confirmed into a public position of responsible action and trust. Becomes very involved in a vocation.

☊ — Same as above.

♈ — Known to be obliging member of cast or group. Cooperative.

☿ — Teaches children. Revises extensively. Writes many drafts to get a perfect copy.

♀ — Gladly will sacrifice for connections.

♂ — Active member of fraternity. Working for a common ideology.

? — Innate shyness. Embarassed by action of associates.

♀ — Executive secretary of state or national lodge or fraternity.

⚼ — Initiation into sorority or fraternity. Lodge of organization.

⚼ — Same as above.

♃ — Accepting an inevitable separation. Leaving with blessings. Undertaking an important step forward.

♄ — To genuflect. To expect or give homage. Deference to one's superior.

)H(— Dislikes disruptions or noises when concentrating.

♅ — Member of ratherstrict religious denomination.

♇ — Ostracizing or excluding aspirant. Political or social boycott.

♃♀ — Serves with family connections.

⊕ — Attempted to clear up old conflicts.

⚡ — Visiting and working around warring tribes.

♈ — Laws which protect only minority groups. Municipal cemetery custodian. Overpowering with associates.

♃Ⅱ — Teaching a few very interested students. Graduate seminar at theological school.

♁ — Loyal organization member. Connected with gruesome accident.

⚟ — Connected with groups concerned with abnormal phenomena. U.F.O. investigators.

♓ — Idealist. Romantic about people.

National tombs. Famous cathedrals. World purge. Abortion.
Ancestor worship. Zealous pioneering. Dedicated. Focused.

M — Known for enduring patience in trying times.

A — Location of meetings or gatherings.

⊙ — Builds on personal strengths and values.

☽ — Respectful of national holidays and family traditions. Builds upon a past for future action. Confines of yesteryear.

♊ — Public memorial service.

♈ — Same as above.

☿ — Scandal widely broadcast. Violence involving a child.

♀ — Gracious reformer. Called for spiritual purity.

♂ — Brutalized by a man.

⚳ — Parents or ancestors involved in well-known violence.

⚶ — Given recognition on annual evaluation. Crowned as empress.

⚴ — Infatuated with worthless husband. Enthusiasm overcomes sense.

⚘ — Same as above.

♃ — Exposed for accepting money falsely. Involved in legal purge.

♄ — Forcibly removed from genetic roots. Relatives abandoned.

♅ — Skillful at exciting others. Sudden death made public.

♆ — Tied to ancient religion. Periods of confusion about goals or aims. Known to have suicidal tendencies.

♇ — Public service. Social servant. Transformation. Going out into the world. Loneliness. Maturing.

⚷ — Respectful person.

⚵ — General cleanup of cemetery. Remodeling the main sanctuary of church or temple.

⚸ — Confinement made international news. Military prisoner.

⚹ — Fired by employer or boss because of eccentric public activities. The state demands sacrifice.

♃♊ — Reflects many cultures. Tracks down events from various periods of time.

♆ — Theories of reincarnation. Advertises regression sessions.

⚴ — Abortion attempt thwarted.

⚹ — World Council of Churches. Gain of faith through death or violence to close relative. Tombs of famous people.

	Restricts communication. Denial of biological children. Students taken away. Unhappily retired from teaching. A single purpose of mind or concentration. Outtalks sex.

M — Often judges before investigating all the facts.

A — Theme of conversation. Repeated solemn vows.

⊙ — Beloved child. Nervous. Ideas. Seminary student.

☽ — Thoughts of ritual archetypes. Rhetoric in old-fashioned cliches. Friendly. Good bedside manner.

☊ — Surrounded by serious literary people and authors. Influenced associates by comments.

♈ — Opinionated. Speaks her mind. Pediatrician.

☿ — Same as above.

♀ — Voices affection or showers gifts on others. Wants to gain emotional security for money. False hopes in love.

♂ — Powerful people and words. Forthright. Pure thought.

⚳ — Raised away from siblings. Isolated during adolescence.

♀ — Author. Documents the growth and behavior of specimen.

⚴ — Period of intense concentration.

⚶ — Same as above.

♃ — Prepared a dissertation along accepted lines.

♄ — Committed to forming opinions. Travels around lecturing about beliefs. Unable to read or write. Kept from studies.

♅ — Innovative but eccentric groups. Concentrates on new concepts. Relates to pain of rare sibling. Argumentative.

♆ — Looking for personal ideals in others.

♇ — Promoted reforms of the organized church. Established Sunday schools. Reform speaker and writer.

⚵ — Shares family with rest of the world. Speaks for modern minority groups.

⚕ — Unethical messages on tape were his undoing. Correcting mistakes. Preserving words of the magician.

⚸ — Quick-on-the-trigger responses. Dangerously tense.

♈ — Inferiority complex caused by domineering father.

♊ — Sensitive to comments. Analyzed diaries or journals.

♏ — Serious activity.

♎ — Sent away from comfortable surroundings of childhood. Thrown into unpleasant situation. Lived among strangers.

♓ — Child taken into isolation. Hears voices from unseen area.

M — Living in a community of segregated women.

A — Often left alone to finish the task at hand.

☉ — Spiritual healing or healer. Zealous defender of causes. Found foster father figure. Docile acceptance of grief.

☽ — Loss of affection. Hurt feelings. Upset digestive system. Loss of daughter. Strong Oedipus complex.

☊ — Glad to sacrifice for friends or acquaintances. Involved with flirtatious women.

♈ — Willing to go out on a limb. Open-minded.

☿ — Serious considerations. Written with great sense of relief and release. Told of old myths and legends.

♀ — Same as above.

♂ — Donates time to fund raising for charities.

♄ — Caretaker of antique treasurer.

♀ — Hard-working. Circumspect banker. Intensely involved in financial dealings.

⚴ — Affections restricted or denied by marital monetary concerns.

↓ — Same as above.

♃ — Pregnant. Multi-talented.

♄ — Mourning widow. Deprived of feminine company. Long period of chastity. Work abounds. Handship unrelieved. Ethical.

⚸ — Aggressive female athlete. Presses to be involved in a truly masculine sport.

♆ — Daughter damaged by drugs or medication. Badly hurt idealistic youth. Remains chaste. Puts females on pedestals.

♇ — Aids severly injured people. Counsels battered women.

⚵ — Ceremonial vocalist. Opera star. Students are his family. Denied normal family and children.

♁ — Death of a loved one or spouse. Deprived of normal growth and maturity.

⚹ — Happiest when working toward a specific goal. Good military career personeel. Strategist.

♈ — Government service. Loves crusading for school bond issue. Excited about involvement in public causes.

♃♊ — Vocalizing the musical scales.

⚻ — Distractions caused fatal mistake. Cheerfully carried out duties to the end.

♎ — Enthused by forceful women. Influenced by dedicated female. Powerful crusader.

♓ — Concerned with religious observances. Adamant about spiritual freedom for all.

↓⚥ / ♂	Eliminates what is unnecessary for the current task. Driven by urge to accomplish. Burns away underbrush. Unusual sexual encounter. Duty before sex. Spell out details.

M — Laborious work. = Neptune, Confusion resulted in death.

A — Fanatic worker. Impoverished family situation. Getting warm beside the hearth.

⊙ — Sensual appearance. Saves energy for important tasks. Good director who gives clear directions.

☽ — Time of committing service. Under strong male domination. Wife of a spoiled brat.

☊ — Associated with political undesirables. Gives lip service. Born during a revolution. Prominent.

♈ — Does not consider responsibilities a burden. Always ready to accept extra pressure.

☿ — Denial of children. Argument or breakup by telephone. Zealous speaker. Dedicated teacher.

♀ — Thrilled by dangerous encounters. Attacked from behind. Prepared for surgery.

♂ — Same as above.

♀ — Quick-tempered in public. Vindictive. Easily bruised. Takes criticism personally. Enjoys stock car racing.

⚨ — Accredited in several areas. Energy involvement. Promotion or title submitted. Learned skills in preparation for job.

⚷ — Received payment for laborious task. Hopping up and down. Unwanted.

↓⚥ — Same as above.

♃ — Opportunities to release attachments. Money changes hands. Strong sense of dedication.

♄ — Security minded. Works hard to achieve precision.

♅ — Sudden accident. Sudden loss of income. Interruptions. Shifting allegiances. Exacting service.

♆ — Confused by sexual encounters. Security washed away. Misunderstood basic urges. Clouded activities.

⚵ — Changes in focus of energy. Basic purpose rechanneled. Puritan ideals challenged.

⚴ — Working together for a cause. Expending energy in group work. Dedicated organizational member.

⊕ — Mass grave. Honoring the unknown soldier or sailor. Layoffs of co-workers.

⚸ — Tremendous recuperative powers. Strong sense of will.

⚶ — Federal or state welfare program. Critical endeavors.

♃Ⅱ — Getting to the core of the problem in chemical research.

⚳ — Delays sex. Caesarean section.

⚼ — Sets up stringent rules for self. Accepts a difficult assignment out of strong sense of duty.

✶ — Religious zealot. Nun who works with the poor.

Following the center path. Compromise with ideas. Evangelist. Ambition thwarted by zeal. Giving service again to the same group or company.

M — Search for ideal religion through organized groups or cults. Possible isolation in convent or monastery.

A — Benevolent servant. Judicious minister. Sober family.

☉ — Divorce. Withdrawal into quiet vacation or retreat alone. Hybrid crop grows.

☽ — Frequently compromises between duty and beliefs.

☊ — Surrounded by religious fanatics or gruff spoken coworkers.

♈ — Took a public stand.

☿ — Serious investigation into a given subject. Loaded down with excessive classes. Kept from friends.

♀ — Jealous of loved one.

♂ — Working for a religious goal. Obsessed. Driven by zealousness. Extremely nervous.

♁ — Being impractical causes disappointment and withdrawals.

♀ — Raising and training horses. Sacrifice much for career.

⚸ — Service oriented person. Severe family dissension. Ritual disfigurement. Nervous reactions.

⚳ — Same as above.

♃ — Same as above.

♄ — Sacrifice for security. Condemns excesses.

♓ — Freed of physical fears. Methodical raising of kundalini.

♆ — Married to medical practice. Impressionable partner.

♇ — Growth of special interest groups. Changing pressures. Opinions being revised by exposure to foreign cultures.

♃ — Belonging to well-known family of social activists.

♁ — A good construction worker.

⚴ — Learn by doing. Control of excessive ambition. Forced to serve a period of menial apprenticeship.

♈ — Learned government prodecure and protocol.

♃ — Service oriented philosophy and culture.

♇ — Imprisoned for upholding own religious principles.

⚷ — Ordained minister.

⚹ — Committed to justice. Enlightened spiritual comprehension. Beyond the physical realm. Ghostly.

107

Warmth within four walls. Self-discipline. Delay in achieving purpose. Assaulted. To tear down or close. Separated. Care for elderly persons.

M — Deep sense of responsibility. Personal pleasure in eventual success following years of sustained effort.

A — Disciplined from an early age. Parents are members of the ministry or priesthood.

☉ — Rather plain in appearance. Dresses in dark and drab colors. dislikes attention to physical looks.

☽ — Ouster of public workers. Menial cleaning jobs around the house or kitchen. Nursing home care.

☊ — Extreme cold weather canceled plans.

♈ — Sent away from home. Abandoned. Deserted. Orphans.

☿ — Mental discipline. Kept silent about pain or damages.

♀ — Separated from loved one because of social pressures. Injury to female sex organs.

♂ — Protective of personal belongings.

♃ — Builds from simple supplies. Lived in a remodeled chicken coop. Hardworking caretaker. Does not complain of hardships.

♀ — Lack of response results in failure. Delayed immune reactions.

⚵ — Rape. Violation of the person.

♅ — Same as above.

♃ — Ambitious to regain status. Overconfidence leads to accidents. Hides insecurities.

♄ — Same as above.

♆ — Sudden death of a minister or nun. Low self-image. Characteristic of a victim or prey.

♆ — Obsession about projects. Confused undertakings. Creates confusion everywhere.

♇ — Forced to accept delays. Subject to great taxation. Upheavals at the hands of others.

⚶ — Austere but loving family life.

⚸ — Works with retarded child.

⚷ — Fights for home and security base.

♈ — Ouster of entire management. Able taskmaster. Compiles government or official statistics.

♃ — Diligent worker. Continues studying throughout lifetime.

⚴ — Conservative and steady. Surrounded by unfortunate individuals.

♉ — Preserves traditions. Zealous supervisor. Vigilance.

♓ — An enduring faith.

108

Naive. Unique goals. Progressive idealist. Intuitive.
Accepts unusual challenges.

M — Zealous adherence to unusual beliefs.

A — Clearly facing relationship changes and challenges.

⊙ — Death by accident. Unexpected challenge from an authority figure. = Pluto, Violent death.

☽ — Driver in car accident which killed mother.

☊☋ — Corrupt explorers. Attracted to powerful connections.

♈ — Challenged in an open and public place.

☿ — Dedicated creative writer. Shares ideas of future. Speaks about "The Great Society." Clever mind.

♀ — Enexpected birth of a daughter. Spasmodic celibacy. Difficult to express affection on personal basis. Worry about proper gift.

♂ — Achieves unusual results. Goes beyond normal states of consciousness. Channels rebellious followers into action.

? — Sudden loss of child.

☿ — Began esoteric study of astrology. Professional metaphysical instructor.

⚕ — Dedicated to changing the inequalities of marriage. Unexpected bindings or restraints.

↓ — Same as above.

♃ — Overdrafts. Fraud. Misapplication of enthusiasm. Not trustworthy.

♄ — Cynical. Tragic circumstances caused by destruction. Poorly understood psychic gift.

♆ — Same as above.

♅ — An idealist. Disillusioned because personal principles failed to gain popular support.

♇ — Breaking down existing barriers and inhibitions. Participate in a psychomotor workshop.

♃♀ — = Sun, Death in an airplane crash.

⊕ — Threatened abortion or miscarriage. Accident or violence for a cause. Purify by changing. Child abuse.

⚹ — The crusading spirit.

⚴ — Received unusual legal powers. Broke years of prior patterns. Authority vested by church and state.

♃Ⅱ — Change in allegiance resulted in further training. Makes some unusual decisions.

⚵ — Ran away from responsibilities. Suicide.

♌ — Not afraid of strange or psychic incidents.

⋇ — Powerful intuition. Warning premonitions.

109

Domestic chaos. Martyr complex. Quarantine. Does not know when to give up. Not seeing goals clearly. Not considering ramifications before acting. Overly zealous.

M — Chronic blood condition.

A — World recovering from a major war. International confusion about directions. Nebulous united efforts and plans.

☉ — False optimism. Expectations unrealized. Disappointed by lack of faith. Pathologist.

☽ — Public propagandist. Congenital condition inherited through the mother.

☊ — Church or synagogue congregation. All-community worship.

♈ — Subservient to wishes of others. Withdrawn manner.

☿ — Guest lecturer. Gives discourses on metaphysical concepts. Double-dealing. Can be vindictive.

♀ — Separation from loved one for reasons not understood by the world. Philosophical about underlying motives. Draws designs.

♂ — Unsettled arguments. Underlying tension.

⚷ — Delivered eulogy for beloved teacher.

♀̣ — Accepted glamour of moving to foreign country. Left security of home to follow a dream.

⚸ — Ceremony of an actor being on stage. Illusion. Operatic performance. Visionary. Mystic.

⚴ — Same as above.

♃ — Luck in perpetuating illusions. Temporary seclusion for religious retreat.

♄ — Express through visual medium.

♅ — Early loss of parental care. Death of mother. Sudden separation for unstated reasons.

♆ — Same as above.

♇ — To give up. Lay everything on the altar. God's servant.

⚵ — End of the line. Last member of the family. Tragedy.

⚳ — Not a beneficial environment. Valiant cleanup of flood damages.

⚶ — Misunderstand one's zealousness.

⚷ — Skilled in diplomacy.

⚴ — Director of metaphysical school. Heads international ashram. Disciple of master teacher.

⚕ — Center of calm in midst of chaos. Puts personal feelings aside in time of need.

⚼ — Anoints others into their ministry.

⚹ — Believes in personal ideals and dreams no matter how unrealistic. Practices positive thinking.

110

Happy to eliminate and regenerate for goals. Brutality.
Frozen plumbing. Isolation from people. Judgmental.

M — Successful businessman due to changes and illness in the family. Went through counseling or analysis.

A — Judges friends and acquaintances.

☉ — Well-preserved body. Hard worker. Stoic. Stalwart. Unmoved by passionate appeals.

☽ — The public shares in transformation.

☊ — Trapped with dying person. Moment of terror connected with strangers.

♈ — Known as an eccentric reformer.

☿ — Forced to correct prejudices or mistaken ideas. Appointment with an analyst. Sexual proposition received.

♀ — Painful medical treatment endured with good cheer.

♂ — Conversion. Tragic loss. Struggle against unjust denials.

⚳ — Undernourished. Vital organs seriously damaged.

⚴ — Career demands many changes in life.

⚵ — Faithful to vows and promises.

⚶ — Same as above.

♃ — Reserved about expressing personal opinions. Reluctant to give interviews with the press.

♄ — Someone removed from life violently.

♅ — Erratic judgment. Spasmodic withdrawals.

♆ — Killed in cold blood.

♇ — Same as above.

♃♀ — Brings startling changes into religious dogma and rituals.

⚷ — Working with disturbed people in isolated location.

⚹ — Not superstitious. Handles change in logical manner.

♈ — Heavy losses through overzealousness. Quarantined.

♃♁ — Undermining of established order. Challenge to current popular philosophy.

⚵ — Miserable in his loneliness. Depression.

☨ — Enforced isolation. Problems to ponder.

♓ — Strong religious traditions. Volatile reaction to accusations. Fervent appeal for religious revival. Answers spirit.

111

Lack of family. Enforced chastity. Death or loss of close relatives. Repossessed house. An only child.

M — Stalwart in face of adversity.

A — Important ancestors but obscure relatives.

☉ — Deprived of active social life. Quiet. Subdued at parties. Constricted. Internal organs not fully matured.

☽ — Sorry to spend time away from wife and children. = Pallas, Sacrifice of family for career caused emotional hurts.

☊ — Associated with many resistance groups.

♈ — In the minority. Lost in the crowd.

☿ — Awarded a fellowship.

♀ — Amiable separation of family to various commitments.

♂ — Concerned with the essence of being.

⚴ — Finds happiness in adopted land.

♀ — Traveled because of career. Employed in time-consuming job.

⚵ — Sudden loss of children. Abrupt change of marital status.

↓ — Same as above.

♃ — Symbolic dream life. Remarriage for sake of the children and elderly parents.

♄ — Father image. Gave up hours from happy family life to fulfill responsibilities. Takes work home.

♅ — Unexpected divorce action. Walks away from excitement.

♆ — Ignored family expectations. Deluded about the future.

♇ — Misunderstandings cause long-term exile from homeland.

⚷ — Same as above.

⚸ — Several family members suffer from terminal illnesses.

⚶ — Lives away from family. Unwanted relative. Pushed aside.

♈ — Divorced from fatherland.

♃♊ — Students like own children. Travel to ancient sites.

⚇ — Death in the immediate family.

⚊ — Extraordinary emotional control.

⚹ — Idealistic marriage or partnership. Couple committed to spiritual work. Trance sessions with mate.

<table>
<tr><td>↓/♀̄</td><td>Scapegoat. Having to cleanup another's mistakes. Nefarious dealings with business partners. Vested interests cared for at other's expense. Bitterness.</td></tr>
</table>

M — An underachiever. Discouraged from reaching goals. Lacking ambition.

A — Sad looking. Shows bitterness and loneliness in expressions.

☉ — Bereaved widow. Born under rather difficult family conditions. Body weakened at birth.

☽ — Emotionally void of ability to respond. Deeply hurt.

☊ — Associated with a religious order which cares for the handicapped and poverty stricken.

♈ — Feels cheated by fate. Lonely person. Heartsick.

☿ — Testified to torture of innocent victims. News of rape and plunder.

♀ — Care of abnormal young woman. Cut off from seers. Abandoning traditional woman's role.

♂ — Processing raw materials or sewage.

⚴ — Works with incubators. Suicidal tendencies. Feels unloved by parents or grandparents. Intestinal problems.

⚵ — Workaholic. Buried under mounds of work.

⚶ — Cut off from own social group. Overly strict with self. Attracts domineering spouse. Married rather late in life.

↓ — Same as above.

♃ — Financed gigantic cleanup campaign for community. Antipollution stand.

♄ — Isolated. Disgraced.

♅ — Unexpected verbal obscenities. Disgusted with immodesty and immorality.

♆ — Vow of obedience. Idealist.

♇ — Obscure condition. Little-known chronic disease. Wasting of body tissue.

⚸ — Religious community. Nun or monk working on social problems. Resurrect a family endeavor or tradition.

♇ — Same as above.

⚷ — Fortress blown up. Vow of poverty. Destruction of security base. Burned the bastion.

↑ — Reacted violently out of feelings of being deprived.

⚳ — Becoming proficient at cleanup assignments.

⚤ — Periodically in the position of being victimized.

☡ — Strong skepticism expressed by agnostic.

⚹ — Lack of reverence for priest. Sincere, hardworking cleric.

113

Zealous worker. Directed power. Youthful folly and adult exuberance show lack of experience in a given area.

M — Gives tremendous energy to accomplish goals. Successful.

A — Civic minded, energetic citizen.

⊙ — Empirical. Power eliminates life force. Killed by lightning.

☽ — Public zeal.

♌ — Military connections. Linked with powerful groups. Mentioned in conjunction with historical leaders.

♈ — Worldwide publication of legal struggle to rectify an injustice. Clarity of thought.

☿ — Charming speaker. Dramatizes his theme when talking. Refutes verbal challenges. Rapid reasoning power.

♀ — Captors treated their prisoners kindly.

♂ — Slow but forceful worker. Good berry picker. Sustained endurance. Lacking in physical stamina.

⚮ — Fight over a gun. Powder burns or gunshot wound. Able to work for long periods of time. Sustained convert.

⚲ — Properly programmed to respond correctly.

⚻ — Careful aim gives a direct hit.

⚻ — Same as above.

♃ — Persuasive crusader. Comprehends great concepts of life. Dedicated to children's care.

♄ — Serious approach is helpful to writer and speaker alike.

♅ — Approaches problems in a roundabout way. Circuitous logic.

♆ — Psychically attuned. Writes of Celtic kings and warriors.

♇ — Inconsistent. Rebels against strong authority. Registered as a conscientious objector.

⚳ — Cleans family grave markers or stones with power tools.

⚴ — Corrupt practices can only be cleared up through legal action. Petition courts to return rightful property.

⚵ — Same as above.

♈ — Leader of underground resistance movement.

⚶ — Persistent. Uses a direct, scientific approach for answers.

⚷ — Clandestine raids. Guerrilla warfare. Harassment.

⚸ — Appears brave in face of social desertion. Staunch support.

⚹ — Prays for success of a crusade. Evangelistic.

114

Mastery achieved through years of discipline and study.
Discriminating. Practical experience added to enthusiasm.

M — Leads in field of choice. Expertise achieved through training.

A — Trusted leader. Respected individual.

☉ — Destined for leadership positions. Fame comes from period of suffering. Showed control and humility.

☽ — Apologized for angry reprimands.

☊ — Religious counselors gather. Hospital chaplain.

♈ — Appointment announced. On the fringe of influence in government.

☿ — A master of rhetoric. Skilled and inspiring orator. Scholar of the classics and ancient Greek.

♀ — Appointed a firm and loyal subordinate to carry out work or orders.

♂ — Arrogance hinders progress. Tried to imitate a stronger, more authoritative man. Responds to flattery.

? — Calmly handled negotiations with employer or superior.

☿ — Good training releases a pupil's innate abilities. Wisely applied discipline.

⚎ — Broken marriage vows or engagement promises.

↓ — Same as above.

♃ — Large area of diseased tissue skillfully removed.

♄ — Achieves through the aid of a superior.

♅ — Brusque movements and words alienate employees or coworkers.

♆ — Questions longstanding concepts of security and allegiance.

♇ — Continued inhibiting of energies.

⚴ — Given legal authority. Leader of the clan. Installed as officer.

⊕ — Poor timing for takeover. Lacks survival know-how.

⚵ — Violence. Surrounded by hostile militia.

♈ — Same as above.

♊ — False self-confidence. Needs inner equilibrium.

⚷ — Overcame severe problems facing them head-on.

⚸ — Breaking through tremendous obstacles.

♓ — Elder statesman among priests and pastors.

| Educated by lifetime experiences. Learned through experience. Necessity brought about changes in career and training. A school of hard knocks. Self-taught.

M — Self-made man or woman.

A — Rather distant with close associates and relatives.

☉ — Involved in commercial deception. Challenge of culture change.

☽ — Sucessful purging of subconscious.

☊ — Constructive confrontations.

♈ — Enjoyed circulating among the educators. Learned through reading and observing superiors.

☿ — Cautious about expressing personal opinions before thoroughly studying an issue or theory.

♀ — Accessible to followers. Capable woman leader.

♂ — Studying toward a teacher's certificate in order to better serve her students' needs.

♃ — Non-partisan stand. Calm in face of rebuffs.

♀ — Adapting to complete cultural change. Coping with loss of modern conveniences.

⚳ — Excels through hours of study and rehearsals.

⚴ — Same as above.

♃ — Respects the old sage. Assertive professor of theology.

♄ — Learned from separations. Studied far from homeland. Education delayed because of unpleasant experiences.

♅ — Accident on return from class. Ideas come from unique study and experiment. Unusual scholarly achievements.

♆ — Minister without a set parish. Teaching and lecturing in various locations. Spiritual leadership demands erratic.

♇ — Creating divisions among the leadership. Upheaval in established procedures.

⚸ — Religious statues and icons. Interested in writing and observing ancient calligraphy techhiques.

⊕ — Accepting the necessity of living in primitive conditions. Learning through major challenges. Archaic procedures.

⚷ — Trained on the job. Won out over others who appeared to be more qualified. Determination.

♈ — Trained a group of executives.

♃ — Same as above.

⚵ — Inexplicably drawn to ancient cultures and civilizations.

⚶ — Finding productive associates. Strong initial impact.

⚹ — Hoped to receive college degree after many years of delay. Spent leisure hours in serious study of ancient philosophies.

116

⚶/⊕	Destruction of traditions and customs of the past. Burying the silver communion vessels. Periods of upheaval.

M — Learning patience and proper timing. Choosing the proper clay or greenware to fire in ceramics work.

A — Needs to learn caution. Wrecks operation in order to build anew. Regrets wrong positions.

☉ — Follows prescribed ritual and positions.

☽ — Dredged up memories of the past. Social snobbery.

☊ — Among the ostracized. Part of religious movement.

♈ — Speaks up for minority stand.

☿ — Adamant spokesperson. Logical mind. One-track thoughts.

♀ — Untimely death of young girl. Disfigurement.

♂ — Agreeing to work under humiliating restrictions. Accepts lowly chores. Violence results in homicide.

⚳ — Salvaging what can be kept of the past.

⚴ — Learned to re-evaluate ancient beliefs.

⚵ — Politely dissects traditional rituals. Taps ancient reservoir of power. Embryology.

⚶ — Same as above.

♃ — Periodic lucky escapes form a pattern for the individual. Optimistic in face of extreme trials.

♄ — Tapped ancient reserves of power.

♅ — Carefully changes old patterns without erasing the secure feelings of traditions. Stable amidst transitions.

♆ — Movies shown in slow motion. Dissolving of longstanding traditions and rituals.

♇ — Upset of universal order no detriment to carrying out aims.

♃♀ — Family breakup.

⊕ — Degradation of the whole moral order of civilization. Spoiled the underlying material form.

⚵ — Fire burns ancestral paraphenalia. Handles problems in a slow and methodical manner.

♆ — Took the struggle to other governments and leaders. Coped with serious legal complications.

♃II — Struggled hard to get necessary training and experience to handle job. Receipt of degree delayed.

⊕ — Same as above.

♆ — Called a "friend of the oppressed." Defended beliefs against mighty odds. Powerful opposition.

⚹ — Scandal touches native's proudest possessions.

Sacrifices are demanded of the native. Multiple duties. Forced to accept positions of responsibility.

M — Guards against hidden deceits. Needs resolution for success.

A — Must learn the difference between excitement and enthusiasm.

⊙ — Unusual family background. Empowered with multiple duties. Appointed to tasks which need much time and dedication.

☽ — Denied maternal love and affection. Early death of mother stifled normal emotional outlets.

☊ — Among enthusiastic people. Able to overcome obstacles by working in unison.

♈ — Public resistance invokes further fights against supposed injustice.

☿ — Newsworthy upheavals.

♀ — Neither scolding or flattery will strongly affect.

♂ — Compulsion to overcome all obstacles. Always prepared for expected dangers. Overly aggressive.

? — Sacrifices made for foster son or daughter. Held virtual captive by close kin.

☿ — Sculpts in clay or glass. Forms and shapes another into desired mold.

⚵ — Wed to career by highest authority. Member of religious order.

↓ — Same as above.

♃ — Willing obedience to religious intervention.

♄ — Unexpected setbacks in struggle for self-control.

♅ — Determined pursuit of new concepts. Unexpected mercy.

♆ — Keeper of sacramental vessels. Altar Guild worker.

♇ — Psychopathic behavior. Perverted sense of justice. Vigilante type action. Indignation against authority.

♃♀ — Complete annihilation of vision.

⊕ — Martyred.

⚹ — Trying all avenues. Mever admitting defeat.

♈ — Accident investigated by government agency.

♃Ⅱ — Educated by varied experiences rather than formal schooling.

⊕ — Sees changes as a cyclic part of natural evolution.

△ — Same as above.

♓ — Led by divine guidance. Somewhat gullible.

118

High ideals. Unrealistic visionary. Illumined. Inspired by myths of old. Legendary hero and heroine.

M — Lives with truth and faith in religious concepts.

A — Impressionable person. Open to suggestion or hypnosis.

☉ — Lives by his or her ideal standards. Pushes the physical body to its limits.

☽ — Seems like a tower of strength to others. Inner faith radiates outward.

☊ — Associated with pastors, priests and rabbis.

♈ — Takes other people on nostalgic journey. Popular visionary.

☿ — Began to utilize writing talents early in life.

♀ — Achieves through determination and intuition.

♂ — Working hand-in-hand with higher consciousness. Concerned with spiritual undercurrents of life.

⚷ — Aquired a stepfather or stepmother.

⚴ — Cripples creativity with monotonous drilling. Suppression.

⚵ — Uplifts sacrament of marriage. Strives toward ideal relations.

⚶ — Same as above.

♃ — Possessing great personal faith. Optimistic in face of serious odds. Recuperative powers.

♄ — Pressed into a desperate situation. Begging for a miracle.

♅ — Exposed original theories of foundation of the universe. Authored contemporary Genesis.

♆ — Has an active and morbid curiosity.

♇ — Converted many. Major move.

⚸ — Preaches about the ideals of perfect brotherhood on earth. Advocate of humanitarian goals.

⚳ — Disappointed in teacher or mentor. Finding the personal dreams (or visions) squelched forever.

⚷ — Pacifist attitude does not exclude sympathy for injured veterans. Willing to completely release control and be directed.

♈ — The gentle leader. Guided by religious principles.

♃♊ — Received doctorate of theology. Learned religious philosopher.

⚴ — Understands escapism.

⚴ — Looking for a superman or super power.

⚸ — Same as above.

119

Appendix A:

PERSONAL POINT CALCULATIONS

In Uranian Astrology certain points within the horoscope are found to link the individual to planetary positions of the day in question, whether it be a birthday or even an eventful day. The German term for these positions is Personal Points which include the Midheaven, the Ascendant, the Aries Point or zero degrees of any cardinal sign, the Moon's North Node, the Sun and the Moon. Newer works and research sometimes include Lilith and the Vertex as Personal Points.

Midheaven relates to the inner ego or the Soul according to the works of Alfred Witte. The German "Ich" fits the meaning of the true person inside the outer skin or personality better than any English translation.

The Ascendant is the addition of others into the personal life related to the German "Du." This includes face-to-face confrontations, intimate friendships, relatives, personal surroundings or relationships.

The Vertex is another locational factor having to do with responses from others. It means roles which are played by the native, involuntary actions toward others or a form of release of activity around the native.

The Aries Point is equal to zero degrees of Aries, Cancer, Capricorn or Libra and connects the native with the world in general. Here are the impersonal relationships of life.

North Node of the Moon from an ephemeris is the position used for Node by Uranian astrologers.[11] It is the connecting link between personal and impersonal worlds. Here are the channels, connectors or ties for the native.

The positions of the Sun, the Moon and Lilith[12] are calculated from their positions in established ephemerides for the exact time of birth.

---

11 The author prefers the true node positions.

12 Positions for Lilith used in this research were from *Lilith, the Doodler*, by Lois Daton.

The Vertex is found in the following method:

90:00:00 degrees of latitude
− _____ birth latitude of the native
= co-latitude of birth

Using the co-latitude of birth, look up the degree of the Midheaven from a table of houses. From this position, determine the degree and sign on the Nadir, or fourth house cusp. The Nadir position is the Vertex, the new Midheaven degree is the Anti-Vertex placement. For example, in a horoscope having a Midheaven of 18 Scorpio 28 with an Ascendant of 28 Capricorn 46 at latitude 35 North the co-latitude would be 55. Thus, the Nadir position would automatically be known as 18 Taurus 28. The Vertex was found to be 0 Virgo 30 from the table of houses.

One of the house systems used by Uranian astrologers is the Meridian. Calculations for finding these positions are given below:

Birth local sidereal time -Midheaven from table _____10th cusp
Birth LST + 2 hours   -Midheaven from table _____11th cusp
Birth LST + 4 hours   -Midheaven from table _____12th cusp
Birth LST + 6 hours   -Midheaven from table _____1st cusp or
                                                    East Point
Birth LST + 8 hours   -Midheaven from table _____2nd cusp
Birth LST + 10 hours   -Midheaven from table _____3rd cusp

For example, a native with a birth LST of 4:54:52 would have the following Meridian house cusps:

10 − 15 Gemini   East Point or 1 − 12 Virgo
11 − 12 Cancer   2 − 15 Libra
12 − 11 Leo   3 − 16 Scorpio

Antiscion, or solstice points, for planets and personal points are used by many Uranian astrologers. A simple plan for calculation of these points is given in Table 9. The base usually considered is the axis between zero degrees of Cancer and zero degrees of Capricorn. Then the principle axis is a mirror image. For example, if Venus is stationed at 12 Cancer, then her antiscion would be 18 Gemini.

Further information about techniques of the Hamburg or Uranian School of Astrology may be found in the various texts on that particular subject.

Sign of Planet	Sign of Antiscion
Capricorn	Sagittarius
Aquarius	Scorpio
Pisces	Libra
Aries	Virgo
Taurus	Leo
Gemini	Cancer

Table 9. Antiscion table for Capricorn-Cancer axis.

Data for the natal horoscope may easily be tabulated in a form like the Natal Horoscope Calculation page to be found in Table 10. Both natal and progressed positions of the traditional planets, asteroids, transneptunian planets, and personal points can be written in the various columns. This is a convenient form designed by the author's husband, Dr. Robert C. Donath, for use with clients and for research.

NATAL HOROSCOPE CALCULATIONS

NAME _____   ADDRESS _____
BIRTHDATE _____   _____
LOCAL TIME _____ GMT ____   TEL: (RES) _____
PLACE _____   (BUS) _____
LAT/LONG _____

	HOUSE CUSPS
S.T. (NOON) (MIDN'T) PRIOR TO BIRTH _____	
TIME ELAPSED TO GMT BIRTH ..... + _____	MC
ACCELERATION OF MEAN SUN ..... + _____	11
SUM............................. _____	12
LONG CORR (– IF WEST, + IF EAST) . _____	ASC
SIDEREAL TIME OF BIRTH .... _____	2
	3

	NATAL	DECL	PROG 19__	DECL	NOTES
☉					
☽					
☿					
♀					
♂					
♃					
♄					
♅					
♆					
♇					
☊					
☋					
☌					
♀					
✳					
⍶					

SOL ARC 19_____
PROG MC _____
PROG ASC _____
DIR ASC _____
East Point _____
VERTEX _____

MOON ECLIPSE BEFORE BIRTH
SUN ECLIPSE BEFORE BIRTH
FULL/NEW MOON BEFORE BIRTH
FULL/NEW MOON AFTER BIRTH

	FIRE	EARTH	AIR	WATER
CAR				
FIX				
MUT				

Table 10.   Simple calculation page.

124

Appendix B:

90 AND 360 DEGREE DIALS

Cosmobiology and Uranian Astrology do not use the traditional house systems. They are both more concerned with the direct relationship of one planet to another. For this purpose the 90-degree and the 360-degree dials are utilized rather than the traditional horoscope wheel.

In using the 90-degree dial, all planets are divided into cardinal, fixed, and mutable elements rather than into zodiacal signs. Thus, all planets falling in Aries, Cancer, Libra or Capricorn are placed in the first 29 degrees of the dial, usually marked with the Aries symbols. The next 30 degrees of the dial, from 30 through 59, are marked with the Taurus symbol and include all planets in the signs of Taurus, Leo, Scorpio and Aquarius. Finally, all mutable signs of Gemini, Virgo, Sagittarius and Pisces are placed in the portion of the dial marked 60 through 89, or the Gemini symbol.

When the planets are in position on the 90-degree dial, all hard or action aspects will be found conjunct each other. Planets in 45-degree or 135-degree aspects will be opposite each other.

One further advantage of both the 90-degree and the 360-degree dial is that midpoints to planets may be found easily. Either use the degree markings around the outer edge of the dial, or use a small inner dial with an arrow, to sight these distances. Specific techniques for use of the dials are found in textbooks on Uranian and cosmobiology instructions.

In the cosmogram, found in Figure 3, regular horoscope placements may be made in the inner circle. The outer circle is for 90-degree dial positions.

Table 11 of arc conversions is a handy tool for placing planets in the 360-degree dial without reference to either sign or house position. Uranian astrologers usually mark the Aries point on the western horizon, as shown.

The 90-degree dial is shown in Figure 4 and the 360-degree example dial is in Figure 5.

Table 11 — Arc conversion table

° OPP. SIGNS	♈	♉	♊	♋	♌	♍	♎	♏	♐	♑	♒	♓
— (0)	—	30 (0)	60 (0)	90 (0)	120 (0)	150 (0)	180 (0)	210 (0)	240 (0)	270 (0)	300 (0)	330 (0)
1	1	31	61	91	121	151	181	211	241	271	301	331
2	2	32	62	92	122	152	182	212	242	272	302	332
3	3	33	63	93	123	153	183	213	243	273	303	333
4	4	34	64	94	124	154	184	214	244	274	304	334
5	5	35	65	95	125	155	185	215	245	275	305	335
6	6	36	66	96	126	156	186	216	246	276	306	336
7	7	37	67	97	127	157	187	217	247	277	307	337
8	8	38	68	98	128	158	188	218	248	278	308	338
9	9	39	69	99	129	159	189	219	249	279	309	339
10	10	40	70	100	130	160	190	220	250	280	310	340
11	11	41	71	101	131	161	191	221	251	281	311	341
12	12	42	72	102	132	162	192	222	252	282	312	342
13	13	43	73	103	133	163	193	223	253	283	313	343
14	14	44	74	104	134	164	194	224	254	284	314	344
15	15	45	75	105	135	165	195	225	255	285	315	345
16	16	46	76	106	136	166	196	226	256	286	316	346
17	17	47	77	107	137	167	197	227	257	287	317	347
18	18	48	78	108	138	168	198	228	258	288	318	348
19	19	49	79	109	139	169	199	229	259	289	319	349
20	20	50	80	110	140	170	200	230	260	290	320	350
21	21	51	81	111	141	171	201	231	261	291	321	351
22	22	52	82	112	142	172	202	232	262	292	322	352
23	23	53	83	113	143	173	203	233	263	293	323	353
24	24	54	84	114	144	174	240	234	264	294	324	354
25	25	55	85	115	145	175	250	235	265	295	325	355
26	26	56	86	116	146	176	206	236	266	296	326	356
27	27	57	87	117	147	177	207	237	267	297	327	357
28	28	58	88	118	148	178	208	238	268	298	328	358
29	29	59	89	119	149	179	209	239	269	299	329	359

Table 11. Arc conversion table.

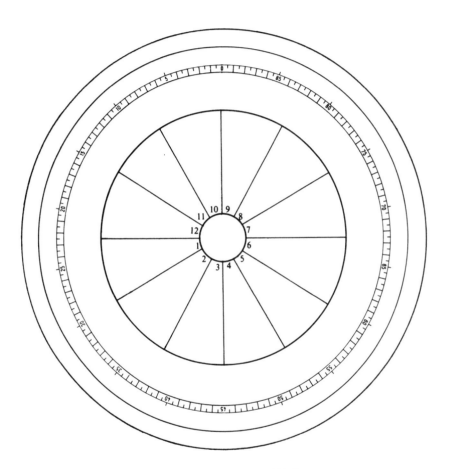

Figure 4.   90-degree Dial.

127

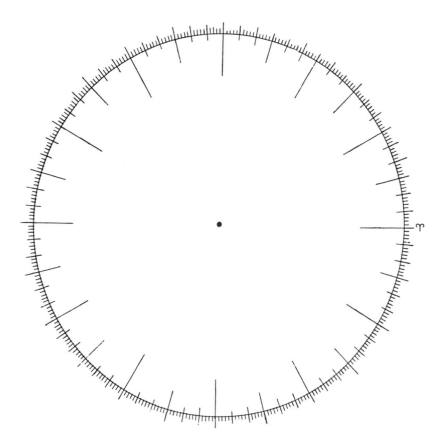

Figure 5.   360-degree Dial.

Appendix C:

AYANAMSA TABLES, 1700-2010 A.D.

Year	Degrees of Difference
1700	20d33m08s
1710	20d41m41s
1720	20d49m46s
1730	20d58m32s
1740	21d06m24s
1750	21d15m20s
1760	21d23m08s
1770	21d32m03s
1780	21d39m54s
1790	21d48m45s
1800	21d56m44s
1810	22d02m24s
1820	22d13m37s
1830	22d21m58s
1840	22d30m29s
1850	22d38m37s
1860	22d47m20s
1870	22d55m15s
1880	22d03m24s
1890	23d12m00s
1900	23d20m54s
1910	23d28m43s
1920	23d37m35s
1930	23d45m34s
1940	23d54m14s
1950	24d02m26s
1960	24d10m52s
1970	24d19m19s
1980	24d27m30s
1990	24d16m12s
2000	24d44m09s
2010	24d53m02s

Table 12.   Ayanamsa conversion table.

To convert the longitude of planets from tropical zodiac to sidereal constellations, the difference caused by the precession of the equinoxes must be considered. These tables give the degrees to be subtracted from the tropical longitude of any planet or point in the horoscope to obtain its sidereal position on the date given. A more thorough analysis of this difference may be obtained from the works of Donald Bradley, Cyril Fagan, Commander Firebrace, Carl Stahl and others.

Calculations were done by Robert C. Donath on March 1, 1979, on a TI-59 Programmable Calculator using Fagan's vernal point conclusions (see Table 12).

CERES —
GODDESS OF THE HARVEST

Animal:	Dolphin — Pigs
Bird:	Dove — Crane
Insect:	Ant
Plant:	Cereal Grains — Corn — Poppies
Emblem:	Scythe — Torch — Sacrificial Knife
Principle:	Nurturing — Healing
Expression:	Cultivation — Harvest — Domestication — Nourishment — Useful labor — Austere beauty — Instinctive racial feelings — Heritage of primitive experience — Initiator of future life — Server — Concern
Manifestation:	Ecology — Cereal grains — Farm tools — Toilet training — Domestic animals and pets — Harvest fairs — Honey — Bread — Caves — Underground Water or Springs
Personification:	British nanny — Servant — Nurse — Nursery school director — — Earth science teacher — Farmer — Salutary Laws — Grandparent — Grandchild

PALLAS ATHENA —
GODDESS OF WISDOM

Animal: Unicorn

Bird: Owl — Cock

Insect: Beetle or Scarab

Plant: Olive Tree — Iris

Emblem: Diamond or Shield — Lance

Principle: Prudent Intelligence — Intuition

Expression: Conservation — Personification of light — Invention — Modesty — Peacemaking — Bravery — Liaison — Insensitive to emotions — Noble mind — Perseverance — Equality in work — Cunning — Skillful Hands — Valour — Perception

Manifestation: Embroidery — Weaving — Job — Flute — Battle Armour — Industry — Numbers — Spinning — Handcrafts — Fulcrum Point

Personification: Weaver — Warrior for peace — Crusader — Patron of arts/crafts — Working women — Counselor — Horse trainer — Sculptor — Librarian — Vocational teacher — National Guardsman — Ombudsman

JUNO —
GODDESS OF MARRIAGE

Animal: Cow

Bird: Peacock and cuckoo

Insect: Bee

Plant: Pomegranate — Roses — Lilies

Emblem: Linked double rings — Sceptre

Principle: Legal mating

Expression: Jealousy — Feminine wiles — In-equality in partnerships or work — Social patterns — Organization in the home — Fidelity — Virtue — Fruitful — Subtlety — Vindictive-ness — Eccentricity — Grace — Mating — Shrewishness — Birth — Quarrelsome

Manifestation: Ceremonies — Weddings — Orna-mentation — Etiquette — Conju-gal honor — Protocol — Mint — Cosmetics — Jewelry

Personification: Bride — Groom — Co-ruler — Co-leader — Vice President — Widow — Hostess — Housekeeper — Guardian of finances — Wife or hus-band — Matron — Yokemaker — Eggs — Sibling

133

VESTA —
GODDESS OF THE HEARTH

Animal: Deer — Donkey

Bird: Nightingale or Ibis

Insect: Spider

Plant: Laurel or oak tree

Emblem: Tripod — Flaming Altar

Principle: Dedication and sacrifice

Expression: Purity — Service — Sacrifice — Solemnity — Chastity — Virginity — Barrenness — Purification — Preserver — Security — Period of servitude — Zealousness — Delay — Warmth

Manifestation: Ceramics — Rituals — Sanctuary — Hearth — Fire — Breaking bread together — Care of ancestors — Altars — Lamps — Houses

Personification: Keeper of traditions — Priests's assistant — Caretaker — Nun or Monk — Acolyte — Altar Guild — Clubwoman or man — Mason — Rosicrucian

CERES
HABITS . . . . NURTURING

PALLAS ATHENA
PATTERNS . . . . PROTECTING

JUNO
CEREMONIES . . . . PERPETUATING

VESTA
RITUALS . . . . PRESERVING

BIBLIOGRAPHY

Ambjornson, Karl H. *Handbook of the 90 Degree Disc.* San Francisco: Ambjornson, 1974.

Bailey, Alice. *Esoteric Astrology.* New York: Lucis Publishing Co., 1951.

Baker, Douglas. *Esoteric Astrology.* Potter's Bar, England: Claregate Publishing, 1978.

DeVore, Nicholas. *Encyclopedia of Astrology.* Totowa, NJ: Littlefield, Adams & Co., 1947.

Ebertin, Reinhold. *The Combination of Stellar Influences.* Freiburg, Germany: Verlag, 1972.

Fagan, Cyril. *Astrological Origins.* St. Paul MN: Llewellyn Publications, 1973.

Greaves, Doris. *Cosmobiology, A Modern Approach to Astrology.* Tempe, AZ: American Federation of Astrologers, Inc., 1980.

Hawkins, John. *Transpluto, or Should We Call Him Bacchus, the Ruler of Taurus?.* Dallas: Hawkins Enterprising Publications, 1976.

Jacobson, Roger. *The Language of Uranian Astrology.* Franksville, WI: Uranian Publications, Inc., 1975.

James, Colin, III. *Relative Strength of Signs and Planets.* Denver: Colorado Astrological Society, Inc., 1978.

Jayne, Charles. *The Unknown Planets.* Monroe, NY: Astrological Bureau, 1974.

Kimmel, Eleanora. *Fundamentals of Cosmobiology.* Denver: Cosmobiology Center, 1977.

Leinbach, Esther. *Planets and Asteroids.* Seattle, WA: Vulcan Books, Inc., 1974.

_____. *Transits.* Seattle, WA: Vulcan Books, Inc., 1977.

Parker, Julie, and Parker, Derek. *The Compleat Astrologer.* Des Plaines, IL: Bantam Books, Inc., 1971.

Reynolds, Jane. *The Life Blueprint.* Glendale, CA: Research Institute of Cosmobiology, Inc., 1978.

Rodden, Lois. *The American Book of Charts.* San Diego, CA: Astro-Computing Service, 1980.

Rudolph, Ludwig. *The Hamburg School of Astrology.* Hamburg, Germany: Witte-Vertag, 1973.

_____. *Rules for Planetary Pictures.* Hamburg, Germany: Witte-Vertag, 1974.

Savalan, Karen Over. *Midpoint Interpretation Simplified.* Tempe, AZ: American Federation of Astrologers, Inc., 1978.

Sherman, Sylvia, and Frank, Jori. *The Uranian Astrology Guide.* West Orange, NJ: American School of Astrology, 1975.